NEVER LOOK AN AMERICAN IN THE EYE

NEVER LOOK AN AMERICAN IN THE EYE

A MEMOIR

✷ ✷ ✷

FLYING TURTLES, COLONIAL GHOSTS,
AND THE MAKING OF A NIGERIAN AMERICAN

OKEY NDIBE

SOHO

Published by
Soho Press, Inc.
853 Broadway
New York, NY 10003

Library of Congress Cataloging-in-Publication Data

Ndibe, Okey, 1960–
Never look an American in the eye : a memoir of flying turtles,
colonial ghosts, and the making of a Nigerian American / Okey Ndibe.

ISBN 978-1-61695-760-5
eISBN 978-1-61695-761-2

1. Ndibe, Okey, 1960– 2. Authors, Nigerian—21st
century—Biography. 3. Novelists, American—21st century—
Biography. 4. Nigerian Americans—Biography. 5. Journalists—United
States—Biography. 7. College teachers—United States—Biography.
8. Nigeria—Civilization—21st century—Anecdotes.
9. United States—Civilization—21st century—Anecdotes. I. Title
PR9387.9.N358 Z46 2016 823'.92—dc23 LC 2016019151

Interior design by Janine Agro, Soho Press, Inc.

Printed in the United States of America

10 9 8 7 6 5 4 3 2 1

For my siblings, John, Ifeoma, JC, and Ogii:
such great fortune to be formed by the clay of C and E!

CONTENTS

1. English Dreams, Communist Fantasies, and American Wrestling   1

2. Never Look an American in the Eye   25

3. My Commission and a Chilly American Reception   37

4. Sleepless in New York   47

5. Nigerian, Going Dutch   57

6. Fitting the Description   71

7. Are You Okay?   83

8. A Norwegian "Okay" Interlude   89

9. On a Croc's Back, America-Bound   95

10. Will Edit for Food   103

11. Lying to Be a Writer   115

12. Writing, Reading, Food, Some Ass Kicking   123

13. A Brand-New American   133

14. An African Folktale, a Wall Street Lesson   149

15. A Dying Father, Dreams of Burma and England   157

16. Wole Soyinka Saves My Christmas   183

17. Crashing a Party, Changing Hearts   195

18. Acknowledgments   209

NEVER LOOK AN AMERICAN IN THE EYE

ENGLISH DREAMS, COMMUNIST FANTASIES, AND AMERICAN WRESTLING

I spent much of my childhood drifting in and out of dreams. Sometimes I pined for a piping-hot plate of pounded yam and egusi soup filled with succulent meat, beef bones with coagulant marrows I could suction into my mouth with just the right sucking action, soft fresh fish that melted on the tongue, and chewy smoked fish or hard stockfish that, one day, I overheard an elder castigate as nutritionless, even though he saluted it for working the dentures to stalwart strength. I dared to dream in the day, wide-eyed, often as I listened to my parents' catechism that a good name, which they had in ample supply, surpassed riches, which they didn't have.

Sometimes, seized by boldness, I disdained dreams of food. Even though I lay on a mat, huddled with my siblings in a cramped room, I entertained no curbs to my dreams. Many a night, ensconced in that room that at times reeked of piss, often from my production line, I fought off the languor of sleep. Awake or half asleep, I prodded myself to turn away from mere matters of food. Instead, I cast my mind to more ambitious planes. Sometimes my fancy would fasten on a car. I would picture myself owning a marvel of an automobile. It was always a Mercedes, a Citroën, or a Volvo. I imagined myself behind the wheel, my hands lightly placed on the steering wheel, the chassis a gleaming wonder, the engine as soft and dainty as the English accent. When the car ran into potholes, it did not whine. Bumps did not shake it, could not speak to it.

Sometimes, I yearned for yet grander escapades. I would block out the symphony of snores that filled the stifling sleep room. Then I would ready myself and soar, off to faraway places.

That was how, sometime just before I entered secondary school in 1973, my itch for America began. America had not been my first childhood dream. Long, long before America, it was England that occupied my dreams. Nor was America even in second place. That position belonged, once upon a time, to the Union of Soviet Socialist Republics (USSR). By the mid-1970s, each of these three foreign addresses seemed to me mythically remote—and, for that reason, alluring. Each enchanted me in its own manner.

In those days, Britain was the country everybody called Obodo Oyibo, the land of the white people. These were the pale people who, years ago, had journeyed by sea from their far-flung land and emerged like ghosts to turn our lives upside down, to conquer and rule us. They represented imperial power. As far as we were concerned, they were the ones who, in Senegalese novelist Cheikh Hamidou Kane's *Ambiguous Adventure*, bewitched the African soul. A major female character in that fine novel seeks to "learn from [Europeans] the art of conquering without being in the right."

For us, the British Isles summed up that other world that lay well beyond the borders of our unsettled lives. It was the world of White magic, White mystery, and White power. If it was said that somebody was traveling to Obodo Oyibo, it was understood by all that the adventurer was headed for Britain. This country was so powerful it had other names: England, the United Kingdom. It had the best of everything in the whole wide world, including the world's two best universities, Oxford and Cambridge. It was said then, in awe, that Britain's two venerable universities were places where, on occasion, a man's head exploded when he tried to read too many books, to stuff too much knowledge into his cranium.

Else, it was said that many an Oxford or a Cambridge man—and occasionally a woman—would sometimes be beset by *isi mgbaka*, an evocative phrase for madness, for the miswired brain.

Beside Britain, every other foreign country was relatively inconsequential, designated by its proper name: America was America, Australia was Australia, France was France, and Germany was Germany. Britain—and Britain alone—was Obodo Oyibo: the white people's country.

I was born in May 1960. That same year, on October 1, Nigeria threw off the British colonial yoke and took on a chic new identity, that of an independent country. Independence, or the pursuit of it, was a hot idea, very much in vogue in the decade of my birth. My experience of Britain, of the British, was essentially abstract in character, much unlike, say, that of my parents.

My paternal grandfather had worked, ever so briefly, as a sawer of wood for British merchants in Nigeria's deltaic region, thickly forested, creek veined. He had quit the job, fed up with his British taskmasters' Olympian flights of rage, their incessant verbal assaults. Despite the brevity of his employment, he picked up a few English invectives, words like "scallywag" and "nincompoop." His pronunciation of the words, which entailed the addition of extra syllables, lent them an archaic edge: "sukaliwagi" for "scallywag," "nimucomupoopu" for "nincompoop." His rather slim harvest of mangled English words inspired the legend that my paternal grandfather was the first person to bring *oyibo*, the English tongue, to his hometown of Amawbia.

My maternal grandfather had had a far-more-enduring relationship with the British. One of the early learners of English, he became versed enough in the strange tongue to earn a job as an interpreter. In those days, interpreters were few and far between. Their facility in Igbo and English translated into tremendous power. They became arbitrators between the conquered but resentful natives and the conquering, haughty colonialists. Many of them raked in fortunes by exploiting their unique position. Interpreters acquired a reputation for corruption. Some of them, for the right inducement, would willfully distort the facts of a case, the better to ensure that the highest bidder became the winner. Those who had cases before British administrators' courts reckoned that victory hardly depended on having the facts on their side. Frequently, the key was to convince an interpreter—with gifts of money, farm produce, or livestock—to shape a case in their favor.

If the British colonial administrators, merchants, and missionaries were to have any form of communication with the native, then the two sides needed the figure of the interpreter, a veritable bridge. Interpreters played an undeniable, essential role. But they were also often characterized in a harsh light. They were deemed to occupy a position of moral dubiety and cultural ambiguity, committed neither to their English masters nor their Igbo brethren but entirely to an illicit desire for lucre. They were sometimes distrusted by the British but prized for the communication they enabled; often feared and despised by their fellow Igbo but nevertheless courted. The Igbo sometimes described an interpreter as that man who could go into the white man's mouth and pluck words from it.

Being in a lucrative post, the interpreter often had access to a harem of women. It was the case with my maternal grandfather, Joseph Odikpo. My maternal grandmother was one of the women who caught his fancy. She had three children for him—two daughters and a son, my mother the oldest.

Unlike my parents and grandparents, I grew up in a world in which the British were a rarity, hardly physically present. In fact, through my secondary-school days, I don't remember any direct interaction with an Englishman or -woman. Even so, Britain and the British exercised a claim on my imagination, on the consciousness of my generation. We read, memorized, and digested textbooks that unabashedly gave credit to the British for discovering every significant geographic landmark in Nigeria, Africa, and the rest of the world. One of them, a Scottish explorer named Mungo Park, had discovered the river Niger, one of Africa's most majestic bodies of water. Even though the river flows through Onitsha, my mother's hometown, it never occurred to me to wonder whether the Africans, who for millennia had lived on the banks of the great river, had all been afflicted with blindness. That questioning would come later, much later, after years of mental awakening, aided by my extracurricular reading of history texts written by Africans, from an unapologetically African perspective.

For years, I had been at peace with the British-told or British-inspired story of my world—indeed of the world, period. Yes, the British body, as such, was not in my face. It was its ghost that my friends and I had to contend with. My uncritical acceptance of the British-fangled account of the world indicated the omnipotence and omnipresence of that ghost. My credulity revealed the sheer scale of British imperial power, even in the decade when I was coming of age.

The British body had receded, but its ghost haunted, menaced, ordered, my world—my classmates' world. One of my classmates in secondary school, whose parents were affluent, spent two or so weeks in London during one of our long breaks. For us, then, London was Britain in microcosm, a city that was the synecdoche of the phenomenal country.

My classmate returned with a mouth filled with amazing tales. Those of us who were luckless, who—as a local phrase went—knew that we would never "smell" London, gravitated to him. His London intoxicated me. I was dazzled by stories of crowds of shoppers milling on streets with rows and rows of fashion stores; of meat and fish shops where there was not a single fly to be seen, everything neatly cut and nicely laid out on glass shelves. I could not get enough. I was desperate to become, through his impressions, a vicarious visitor to the very center of Obodo Oyibo. He had bathed

in the rose-tinged perfume of London. His stories brought me some
of the city's whiff and transcendent touch.

In fact, by going to London, he'd made himself, in my estimation, a figure of History. He was the equal of the Scottish adventurer
Mungo Park. Park had discovered a great river in my backyard; my
classmate had discovered London!

I joined the coterie of the curious who stalked the discoverer,
pestered him with questions. I was not the only one who, at every
opportunity, rephrased the one question he'd been asked, the same
question he'd answered numerous times. *How, what, was London
like?* There was something monochrome about the discoverer's
answers, but we didn't care. We were caught in a frenzy of curiosity; London and all it represented made us giddy, bewitched.

"You've never seen a place like it," the one who had touched and
smelled London would begin; a London-inspired half smile would
etch itself on his face. Even in their prosaic ordinariness, his words
conveyed something of the sheer dazzle of London, confirmed our
sense of a city that exuded an air of calm and charm, composure and
enchantment. "Everywhere you look, as far as your eyes can go, all
you see is concrete. There's no patch of grass in London. In fact, you
can't see any sprout of grass."

That picture of an infinitely paved landscape struck me. It cast
a spell over me, stayed branded on my mind for years, even past the
time when it dawned on me, finally, that it was a false, concocted
portrait. All these years later, even after I had made several visits to
London, after I had beheld the city's tree-lined streets and tree-rich
parks, after I had seen the English countryside in the summer, with
its verdant hillocks and endless rolling greenery, my classmate's
first portrait still has a vestigial fascination. To this day, a part of
me still holds out hope of taking a turn someday on a visit to London and stumbling on an unyielding, relentless carpet of concrete.

For sure, in those days, grass and trees were part of our shame.
They accused us as inhabitants of accursed Africa. They spelled our

lives as "bush" people. They connoted the absence of "civilization," meant that we were "native" and backward. Grass and trees marked us as primitives who lived in a state of nature. To me and, doubtless, to many of my classmates, a landscape that was grassless and treeless, covered in concrete, was the epitome of civilized glory. I couldn't wait to escape my shrubs and trees, to land in London's flora-denuded paradise, to waltz on London's plastered streets, and, if I wished, to lie down and roll over and over on that eerie, endless stretch of concrete. (Along with that dream came a desire to savor Obodo Oyibo's canned delicacies, instead of the pot-cooked meals I was condemned to eat, often with my fingers.)

My father, Christopher Chidebe Ndibe—CC to his friends—added to my fascination with Britain. One reason was that he had an English friend, Reverend John Tucker, with whom he exchanged letters and postcards several times a year. To me, Tucker was as mysterious as his country—and every bit as alluring. I couldn't conjecture who he was, or reckon how and where my father had met him. And it wasn't easy to ask, either. I grew up at a time and in a world where children could not march up to adults with personal questions. Children did not pry into adult affairs. The incautious, overcurious child was liable to get a hard knock or two on the head, delivered with the nub of clenched fists, a slap with the open hand, or a few sizzling "corrective" strokes delivered on the buttocks with a sturdy cane. Asking my father about his English friend was out of the question.

In a sense, it was all for the better. As I knew next to nothing about Tucker, he became putty in the service of my fantasies. I could mold him into any shape I wished; I could knead him to suit the twisting contours of my dream. And there was no question that he occupied an extraordinary spot in my life.

My father was a postal clerk, my mother a schoolteacher. They were altogether too poor to take my four siblings and me on vacation anywhere, much less to London. I had to make do with Tucker.

Since Father had a friend in Obodo Oyibo, I permitted myself to fantasize that I had ties, however tenuous, to that famed location called Britain. Tucker "snuck" me into Britain; he became my unsteady grasp on a fragile, slipping dream.

A British fetish accompanied Father's shaving routine. Each morning, he shaved on the veranda of our country home. Chin raised, lips sucked in, hand guiding a razor in a delicate motion up and down his lathered cheeks, Father had his small transistor radio tuned to the World News Service of the British Broadcasting Corporation (BBC).

For me, the radio was a thing of inscrutable magic. I remember it as one of the first objects to strike me with awe. At first, I imagined that the newscaster was some kind of mysterious being, contorted in shape and miniaturized to fit into that radio. How did the white man manage that amazing feat? At some point, of course, I realized that the speaker was not inside that metallic box. Yet, far from settling the mystery, the realization deepened it. How did these white people conjure up the marvel of planting words that spun and sped in the air through thousands of miles in order to resound in my father's radio?

I wondered whether some people had the wizard eyes to see the words as they floated in the air, all the way from London, to my hometown. Surely Indians, renowned for their talismans, would have those special eyes that saw things invisible to the ordinary eye. In my days of youth, India was the world capital of magic and wizardry. Adults said Indian athletes had been banned from the Olympics because they had talismans that enabled them to defy time, gravity, and height. In any track contest, the Indian athlete would appear at the finish line the instant the whistle went off. Indian high jumpers could clear any height, even as high as a skyscraper. As for the pole vault, Indian jumpers could vault themselves high above the clouds. Their swimmers could swim from one end of the pool to the other in—literally—no time. Nigerian newspapers and magazines carried advertising featuring a variety of Indian shamans and gurus. I recall that each shaman sat cross-legged, face and bare upper body elaborately painted, a serpent curled around the neck, a staff curlicue in one hand. The advertisement vended potions, talismans, and elixirs. If you desired any woman's affection, there was a romantic potion called Touch-and-Follow. All you had to do was smear the ointment on your palms, draw close to the object of your desire, and touch her. She'd abandon everything, forsake everybody else, and follow you. It was that simple: guaranteed. If you had an exam, there was some talisman to enable you to score perfect marks. It made the answers appear on the palm of your hand. You just copied the answers from palm to paper. And, just like that, you soared to great triumph, guaranteed. If your heart ached for riches, why, the Indian shamans had just the code to bring a shower of cash into your life. If you wanted a third eye, to see far beyond your fellows, to behold the mysteries and secrets of the spiritual realm, there was just that Indian-made formula to help you acquire it.

Surely, a people who had conquered distance and mastered time could see words spoken in London, floating in the spheres, headed for Father's radio. How come these Indian seers were never tempted to reach in the air and snatch up the flying, tumbling voices?

For me, it all meant that the magicians of Obodo Oyibo were more versed, equipped with far more spellbinding skills, than those of India. And if the inhabitants of Obodo Oyibo could pull off the wonder of words in the air, what other tricks could they play, what other spells cast?

I would—I could—find out if I ever had the chance of landing in Concrete London. So I yearned for London.

Then, one fateful day, the Union of Soviet Socialist Republics blasted into my childhood dreams and seized center stage.

As a child, I was something of an expert eavesdropper. If I spied any group of adults who seemed engaged in heated or juicy conversation, I'd stake out a position near them. There was an art to it. I could not afford to let on that I was there to fish snippets from adults' conversation. If I got caught at it, I knew I would be sharply rebuked or even smacked. The trick was to be at once near and unobtrusive, to steer within hearing range but give the impression of being occupied with something else.

One day, I saw some men in a bar, drinking and eating and talking animatedly. I drew near enough to overhear them but also pretended to focus on kicking around a makeshift soccer ball spun from rags.

"So, tell me more about this thing you call comanizim," one of the men said, addressing a man whose face bore a thick, bushy beard.

"Communism," the bearded man corrected.

"Eheh, tell me more about this comanizim," the first man demanded.

"Communism means that people own everything in common. Everything! There's nothing like *This is my own* or *That belongs to me*. And you can't hear it said that this man is rich, that one poor. Everybody is equal in communism."

"But they must have rulers," interjected the first speaker.

"Yes, but the rulers are in truth the servants of the people."

"Surely, the rulers have big houses reserved only for their use. And big cars they alone ride in."

"Not under communism!" the bearded one assured. "It doesn't matter who you are, once you feel the call of sleep, you can walk into any big house, look for the biggest room, lie down in the biggest bed—and sleep. Yes! The first to claim a big bed gets to sleep in it for the night. There's no argument about it. If a ruler happens to walk in late, he may end up with the smallest bed. And he won't make a fuss or demand that the person in the big bed get up for him. No!"

"But what if one person takes a key and locks a big house so he alone can enter it?"

"Impossible!" shouted the bearded fellow. "In fact, it's against the law to lock any house. It's also against the law to lock a car. The key is always left in every car's ignition. If you want to drive to some place, you open the door of any car, start it, and drive away. It doesn't matter if the car is a Rolls-Royce. Each car, even the most expensive one, is as much yours as anybody else's. All cars are owned in common."

"This comanizim is very good," one of the other drinkers said.

"Communism," the bearded man corrected again. "That's why we workers are fighting to make this country a Communist one."

My heart beat riotously. I, too, was willing to fight to bring communism into our lives. Born poor, I badly wanted my circumstances leveled *up*. I felt a strong stirring inside to know what, from a distance, seemed to me the luxurious life of my acquaintances whose parents had cars. I fantasized about riding with my parents in a different car each day, sleeping in a different big house—a mansion—each night. I'd make sure, I resolved in the silence of my heart, always to stake out the most rare cars and to beat everybody, night after night, to the softest, biggest bed in the swankiest homes.

A chance encounter with the words of that bearded man was all it took to transform me into a Communist! The man's cause became mine. For a moment, I felt tempted to walk up to the men and announce my enlistment in the fight for Communism. I refrained only from fear that such an impetuous gesture might jinx things.

At the time, my parents had never owned a car, any car. Years later, having qualified for a loan from the state government, my mother bought a Peugeot 404 that became my parents' one and only car. I hadn't had the fortune of sleeping in a bed. Each night, my siblings and I brought out rolled up raffia mats, unfurled and lay them on the hard floor, and went to sleep. A few folded shirts served for pillows. My childhood dreams never wandered to the remote territory of cars or even soft mattresses; they hovered around food.

"If you succeed in bringing this comanizim—" one man began to ask.

"It's not if, it's when," the bearded one interjected. "The struggle of the workers always succeeds."

"I can own a car, then—when you succeed?"

"And I, a big house?" another man asked.

"No," the bearded man answered exasperatedly. "Didn't you hear me say that nobody owns *this* or *that*?"

"But you said poor people in comanizim own big cars and mansions," one of the men challenged.

"No, they don't own. The community owns everything in common. That's what I said, unless you're drunk already. Everybody can *use* what is owned in common."

His audience fell silent, seemed to weigh his words. Then one of them asked, "Who thought up this idea?"

"A man called Karl Marx," answered the bearded man, dragging out the name. "My beard is nothing compared to his. There was no knowledge in this world that he didn't have in his head."

"Kalu Mazi," one of the men said, pronouncing it as an Igbo name.

"No, Karl Marx."

Karl Marx or Kalu Mazi, I loved this man who had invented this thing called communism. I pictured a human head filled to the brim with knowledge. It made sense to me. Here, after all, was a man who'd devised a system that offered everybody access to plentiful food, access to cars, big beds, and mansions. Communism meant, for me, the very extinction of poverty.

I knew what communism meant, knew who invented it, but there remained a mystery: Where was it to be found? For unless it existed somewhere, it was all a fairy tale, airy.

The conversation progressed. Then, as if he read my agitation, one of the men let out a sharp excited whistle, filliped his fingers, and asked whether there was anywhere in the world where communism had been planted.

"Several places," said the bearded man. He named Cuba, which didn't sound to my ears like a country. He named China, which somehow didn't impress me. Then he said, "There's the Union of Soviet Socialist Republics, USSR."

Perhaps it had to do with the sheer flourish of the name, capped with that acronym, USSR, but somehow the name clicked! That day, the USSR matched—perhaps even supplanted—Britain as the place in the world I most wanted to visit.

Just when I thought the matter settled, America sneaked up on me, announced itself into my dreams, and made a claim for my attention I was powerless to resist. America didn't come with anything that rivaled Britain's ornate charms; it lacked that primal prestige that belonged alone to that veritable Obodo Oyibo. Nor could it boast that sunny Communist paradise that elevated the USSR. It was its mixture of swashbuckling drama and flair for evocative names that compelled my attention.

It all began during a school vacation I spent at the home of relatives who lived in Enugu, the then capital of East Central State. My hosts' mammoth black-and-white TV set ran a steady parade of American programs. Bewitched, I sat for hours in front of that TV. There were episodes of *Gunsmoke* and *The Mary Tyler Moore Show.* Yet, it was American professional wrestling that seized me by the scruff.

They had names like Jimmy "Superfly" Snuka, Ricky "the Dragon" Steamboat, Ernie Ladd, Mil Máscaras, Wahoo McDaniel, Mighty Igor, André the Giant, Pedro Morales, "Nature Boy" Buddy Rogers, Terry Funk, Bruno Sammartino, Chief Jay Strongbow, Superstar Billy Graham, Harley Race, and Big John Studd. I was blind then to the secret that wrestling matches were often choreographed, the outcomes fixed. I marveled at the drop kicks, pile drives, body slams, head butts, figure-four leg locks, and a variety of submission holds. The wrestlers had to be a different breed of men, specimens grown on some human farm, their bodies steel-like. I pictured each of them devouring two whole chickens at a sitting, wolfing a whole pot of rice. How else could they fly from the top rope and slam their bodies on an opponent lying supine in the ring? How else could the slammed wrestler survive the crush of that massive weight coming at such velocity?

The wrestlers' rhetoric was an art in itself. It grabbed my attention. With tubular arms, they stabbed the air. They threatened to break their opponents limb by limb, or vowed to put them in the hospital, to drive them into forced retirement. It was spectacular theater, except that I didn't have that name for it at the time.

I couldn't get over the wrestlers' sheer bigness, how some of them looked like two or three men glued together. It stirred something within me, a desire to see America, the country that produced these elephantine beings.

Back in my hometown, I told all my friends about these amazing men I had seen on TV. I demonstrated some of the wrestlers' moves and invited them to practice on me. In one session, a friend twisted my arm so hard that a wristbone popped out of place. I kept the injury and the pain secret, scared to tell my parents. Through pain, through mimicry of American wrestlers, the United States surreptitiously burrowed its way into my dreams.

As I paid attention to America, I became fascinated by the names of its actors, its cities and states. In my secondary-school days, a kind of chewing gum was in vogue. Each pack of gum came with a small card that bore the name of an American actor. You unwrapped the gum and saw a card with the name and photo of, say, Lorne Greene or Dan Blocker. One day, I unveiled a card with the photo and name of Tony Curtis. I believe he had two guns.

My parents had named me Anthony, after Saint Anthony of Padua. The moment I saw the card, I renamed myself Tony Curtis.

It became my reigning name throughout my secondary-school years and gave me a newfound swagger that went with a wild, awakening interest in girls. A part of me adored the country that had sent me this new, heady, gun-flaunting name. There was a strange music to it, the same way other "American" names had captivated me and many other youngsters of my generation. Many of my secondary-school mates adopted North American names, won over by their unusual sound. One friend took Alabama, another Manitoba, yet another Lorne Greene. There was an Adam Faith and an Arizona. I was thrilled by the sound of Tennessee and Mississippi; I couldn't wait to visit them.

My relationship with America evolved, entered a mature phase, a year after I gained admission into Yaba College of Technology in Lagos to study business administration. I was still a devotee of American professional wrestlers, but by happenstance—browsing an outdoor bookstore at Yaba Market—I discovered books by or on Martin Luther King Jr. and Booker T. Washington, and novels by several American writers, white and black—Richard Wright, John Steinbeck, Ralph Ellison, Ernest Hemingway, James Baldwin. These books extended my earlier interest in North America sparked by reading *Time* and *Newsweek* magazines that my father often bought. I began to explore the world through these American texts, delving ever deeper into matters Americana. Some of the readings exposed me to the horrors faced by Africans taken captive and enslaved in the so-called New World. I took pride in accounts of these captives' mighty struggle for liberation. The more I read, the more baffled I became—but the more drawn I felt to America.

The books and journalism I consumed fueled my desire to write. I needed writing badly, needed it to save me from a career in the corporate world that my studies would sentence me to. Bohemian at heart and by habit, I dreaded the prospect of a regular eight-to-five job. Even more frightening was the idea of perennially sporting a tie—an altogether bizarre invention of male fashion that

I have never understood or cared for. I began to send out opinion pieces to several Nigerian newspapers. My confidence grew with each piece that got published. At graduation I had made a modest name for myself—enough to earn me job offers from several newspaper groups. Journalism suited my restlessness and knack for adventure. After a two-year stint at the Concord Group of newspapers, I accepted an offer as an assistant editor at *African Guardian*, a Lagos-based weekly newsmagazine.

One day, in September of 1988, the editor's secretary hailed me as I arrived at work.

"Oga Okey," he said, "Professor Chinua Achebe called you from America."

The palpable glee in the secretary's demeanor was understandable. Achebe was one of Nigeria's biggest cultural icons, a fact known even to those Nigerians who hardly read books. He had become a world-class novelist, his *Things Fall Apart* belonging to a select body of books that had a significant global readership. At the time, he held a distinguished visiting professorship at the University of Massachusetts Amherst. He would often call me when he planned to arrive in Nigeria. With his eldest son, Ike, I would go to the international airport to welcome him.

My relationship with him had had an interesting evolution.

The first time I ever saw Achebe was in 1976, the year before I completed secondary school. My set had had the luck of coming along just as a major curricular shift was taking shape. After decades of being disdained, Africa was finally incorporated into secondary-school curriculums. African history replaced British and European, and African literature unseated the former focus on (very) English literature. Where those who preceded my set had studied such writers as Thomas Hardy, Charles Dickens, Emily Brontë, and Charlotte Brontë, my classmates and I were assigned books by Achebe, Wole Soyinka, Ngũgĩ wa Thiong'o (who then went by James Ngũgĩ), Kwesi Brew, Cyprian Ekwensi, Robert Wellesley Cole, and Kofi

Awoonor (then known as George Awoonor-Williams). Most of the titles we studied were published in Heinemann's African Writers Series, the photo of the author on the back cover of the orange-colored books.

During the long vacation, some of my friends and I would occasionally gather at a spot in the town of Enugwu Ukwu beside a busy road that connected Enugu, the state capital, with Onitsha, the famed commercial town on the banks of the River Niger. It was one of several locations where cliques of youngsters would congregate. We'd talk *jazz*—which meant any subject that caught our teenage fancy. We'd steal puffs on cigarettes. We'd take furtive swills of *kai-kai*, the fiery, locally brewed gin that set the mouth's roof on fire. We'd wince as the liquid scalded its way down our brave, shuddering esophagi. Most of all, we'd just stand around, dawdle, idle away time. What we wanted, rather desperately, was adventure. We'd scavenge for any excitement to spice up our lives, anything that would deliver us from the curse of too much time, too little to do. We were bored, for sure, to hell and back, even though we didn't know it at the time. Nobody had given the word "boredom" to the agitation we felt, the restlessness within. And if anybody had attempted to sell us the theory, we would not have bought it at any price—we simply didn't have boredom in our social dictionaries.

On a Saturday, as we stood around, one of us sighted a blue unusual-shaped car that shook off a slight bend in the road and unfurled itself, headed in our direction. It may have been some silent transmission of urgency in the first observer's gaze, or perhaps he rallied us with words; I no longer recall. But the curious, strange automobile—curious as to color, strange as to shape and type—became the cynosure of all our eyes. In a moment, as the speeding long-bodied car whirred past, we fixed on the driver. We'd never seen that make of car ever before. But its driver was immediately recognizable. Instantly, from the driver's resemblance to the author photo on the back of *Things Fall Apart,* we recognized Chinua Achebe!

A few of us jumped onto the paved thoroughfare, indifferent to the danger from other traffic, and waved frantically. We saw him see us from his rearview mirror and saw him raise a hand to return our greeting. Our eyes had beheld a legend. We had a stock of excitement to last us a week.

Subsequently, we staked out the same spot every Saturday, expectant. Time and again, our vigil was rewarded. Once we spied the car from a distance, we'd start waving way before Achebe drove past. He'd make eye contact with us, smile in that accustomed wry way that I would come to recognize, a few years later, as his signature, and wave to us. Each time he drove past and waved at us, we felt our lives touched by magic, our week made.

One day, during a solitary walk, I chanced upon Achebe. He'd stopped at a gas station to fuel up his blue Mercury Monarch. My heart skipped a few beats at the sight of the legend. I walked toward him in the slow, timid steps of one approaching a god of unpredictable temper. Should I speak to him? Say what, exactly? Tell him I had been enchanted by his work? Or should I exhibit (puny) erudition? Ask him a question or two about, say, the impulsive, domineering Okonkwo in *Things Fall Apart,* whose killing of the boy Ikemefuna shook me to my very depths, gave me one of my earliest, purest portraits of evil? Or should I ask about Obi Okonkwo, the self-willed, failed idealist protagonist of *No Longer at Ease?* But what if Achebe upturned the scale, asked me a question or two about his novels? What then? Could I find words to give a coherent answer? Or would dread be a boa constrictor around my throat, stifle every word welling up for air, nervousness choke each word to death? What if Achebe knew he was a deity in my eyes, and that eminent personages like him didn't have to speak to mere mortals—least of all, an upstart, uppity, secondary-school mortal? What if he ignored me, if he stared or glared at me in silence?

Once within earshot, I blurted out—the only words, ultimately, my breath could form—"Good afternoon, sir."

"Good afternoon," Achebe said in response. The surprise softness of his voice put me at ease. Then, as if to garnish the gift of returning my greeting, he humored me with a smile.

I lingered until he finished fueling, entered his car, and drove away. Then I ran, panting, to a friend's home. I knew that a few other friends of mine would be there, too. In an urgent, even agitated, tone, I related what had just happened, my close-up encounter with the writer whose quick wave had become for us the crowning thrill of many a weekend. My friends moped at me, their expressions a mixture of awe and envy. They knew what I felt: that my life had been brushed by stardom.

Still giddy, I served notice to my friends. Since the great Achebe had not only acknowledged my greeting but had also returned it—with a smile, to boot—I let my friends know that, for the next two weeks or more, I would not use the same mouth that saluted Achebe to talk to insignificant people like themselves!

It was years before I spoke to Achebe again, in circumstances that were far more amazing.

It was 1983. I had just graduated from college and been hired as a staff correspondent by the Lagos-based *African Concord*, my first job in journalism. Before taking up the post, I traveled to Amawbia to share the news with my parents and to receive their blessing. I also visited Ogidi, Achebe's hometown, to see a friend. As we conversed, I raved and raved about Achebe and *Things Fall Apart*. I confessed to envying her for belonging to the same town as the famous writer. The young woman listened for a while, her cheeks stretched in a smile. Then she asked, "Do you know that Achebe is my uncle?"

"He is?" I said in surprise.

"And his house is a short walk away."

"Really?"

"And he's home this weekend. Do you want us to go visit him?"
Did I ever!

The Achebe I met in his country home personified grace.
He welcomed us in that quiet, warm manner that was his style. He
served us tea biscuits and chilled Coca-Cola. He fixed me with
penetrating eyes as I gushed about his novels, his short stories,
his essays, even reciting favorite lines memorized from years of
devoted reading. He asked a few questions of me, and I felt flattered by his attention as I spoke. Before taking leave of him, I
related that I had recently been hired by *African Concord*. Would
he agree to an interview with him for the magazine? Ever gracious, he consented. He gave me his home telephone number at
the University of Nigeria, Nsukka (UNN). I should simply give
him a ring whenever I was ready.

A week later I flew to Lagos, reported for work, and told Lewis
Obi, the weekly magazine's editor, that I had Achebe's telephone
number—and a standing commitment to give me an interview.
The editor was elated.

"That will be your first major assignment," the editor said. The
interview, he added, would be the magazine's cover story.

I rang Achebe to set a date for the interview. The magazine
made arrangements for my flight from Lagos to Enugu, the nearest
city to the writer's location. On the scheduled date, the author and
I met at his spare, book-lined office at the university's Institute
of African Studies. The very air seemed flavored with the scent of
books stretching and heaving. An air conditioner droned, ineffec-
tual against the humid heat.

Pleasantries quickly exchanged, I pressed the RECORD button
of my tape recorder. A minute or so into the interview I paused
and rewound the tape to check that everything was working. Satisfied, I continued the interview. I asked questions about Achebe's
fiction, poetry, and essays, about literary politics, and about Nigeria's vexed current affairs. He responded in his deliberate, accessible

language. He spoke softly, for the most part, as if words were fragile things liable to shatter should he raise his voice. Yet, raise his voice he sometimes did. At moments, his voice rose, accentuated. His words, like ripples, rode the surface of his soft, even voice.

Three hours later, rather reluctantly, I rose to take leave of him.

"This is the most exhaustive interview I have ever done," Achebe remarked. "Where did you study literature?"

He was surprised to learn that I had read business administration at Yaba College of Technology in Lagos and the Institute of Management and Technology (IMT) in Enugu. He laughed when I described myself as a certified misfit and shirker as a business student.

I had been a sartorial oddity both at Yaba Tech and IMT. Fellow students majoring in business administration sported overpolished black or brown shoes and wore dress shirts and ties. I had drifted about campus in jeans, T-shirts, and mud-caked sneakers. While other students pored over business and accountancy texts, I had indulged my fondness for reading novels, magazines, and newspapers, local as well as foreign. While they crammed accounting principles and filled their heads with labor laws, I had imbibed the works of Soyinka, Ngũgĩ, Achebe, Okigbo, Flora Nwapa, John Steinbeck, Kofi Awoonor, Jane Austen, Armah, Buchi Emecheta, the Brontë sisters, Richard Wright, William Faulkner—and had memorized lines from *Time* magazine essays by Lance Morrow and Roger Rosenblatt. Forsaking business texts—except for the two or three days before exams—I had fervently followed the controversies and feuds that often erupted between writers in Africa and elsewhere.

A few friends were waiting for me at Hotel Presidential Enugu, where I was lodged, when I arrived from interviewing Achebe. They were eager to listen to Achebe's voice. Happy to oblige them, I fetched the tape recorder and pressed PLAY. We waited—not a word! I put in two other tapes, the same futile result. Each tape rolled but produced only a steady whir and soft wheeze, not a word Achebe had spoken. How was I going to explain this mishap to my editor—who had scheduled the interview as a forthcoming cover?

Terror seized me. I had not taken a single note throughout the interview. Why, I had had no inkling that technology could turn merciless saboteur. Until then, it had not crossed my mind that a tape recorder could be so fickle, so inept, could sleep on duty. At any rate, I had checked that one time, at the beginning of the interview, and the tape recorder had seemed fine. Now, there was nothing to show for all my effort, all the time I had put in. I asked the hotel's switchboard to ring the writer's home for me. When Achebe picked up, I panicked, for a fleeting moment too flustered to find words. Then the words came in a torrent.

"Professor, this is Okey. Okey Ndibe. I don't know how to explain this. I owe you a big apology. I'm so sorry I wasted a lot of your time today. I don't know what happened, but my tape recorder did not work. You remember I checked once and it was working. But everything seemed to have stopped after that. I should have checked periodically. The recorder didn't catch even one word you spoke."

I paused, to let him absorb the astonishing information. When I was growing up, my parents often caned me when I broke chinaware or screwed up in some other way. Caning was a painful but neat way to put a closure on things. The dose of pain marked each errant moment and then released me to move on with my life—until I broke something else, screwed up another time. Cane-inflicted pain was its own form of vocabulary. It gave the body a language with which to inscribe failure, to etch the memory of a lapse—and then to file it away. On the phone with Achebe, a part of me wished he would voice fuming, flagellant words. I wished he'd berate me for my lack of fastidiousness, my lack of diligence. Let him scold me as much as he wanted, but let him not foreclose a second chance. Let him not hang up, leaving me to stew in my distress.

"Oh, so sorry to hear that," he said calmly, nary a note of exasperation or impatience in his tone.

It was a wonderful surprise, his tone. Yet, it would take more than a patient, sympathetic tone to dispel my discomfiture. There was no question: should I return to Lagos without accomplishing my task—without the interview—my career as a journalist would be as good as over. It would be stillborn, dead on arrival. And there was no other way I had ever wanted to make a living.

"I'm so sorry," I repeated.

"No, not at all," Achebe said. "These things happen."

"I'll be fired if I go back with nothing. Could I come back tomorrow for a short interview? Thirty minutes—even twenty— would do," I pleaded.

"Not tomorrow," he said. "I have a full day. But if you can come the day after, I'll give you all the time."

Two days later, I arrived in Nsukka for the salvage interview. This time, I went with three tape recorders. I also took copious notes, prepared for technology's capriciousness, mischief, and malice. Achebe was as indulgent as the first time. He was genial as he answered all the questions I threw at him. I paused every few minutes to check that the three recorders were working. I had stretched the interview to an hour and a half before guilt—mixed with gratitude—compelled me to stop.

But I made sure to ask a question that went to the heart of Achebe's trademark style. He was famous for a spare narrative style that shunned any form of linguistic contortion, adornment, or flashiness. I asked him about it. He explained that he was not fond of writers who use language to confound readers. Invoking the example of the philosopher-mathematician Bertrand Russell, he explained that true mastery of any discipline did not lie in using jargon to keep the uninitiated at bay. A true expert, instead, was one who understood a subject well enough to make its most intricate concepts accessible to a novice.

The second interview was not as exhaustive as the first one, nor did it have the spontaneity of the first outing, but it gave me—and the readers of the magazine—a prized harvest. My friends got a chance to savor Achebe's voice, with its mix of faint lisps and accentuated locutions.

Few writers of his stature would have sacrificed so much of their precious time in an interview with a rookie journalist. He had saved my career.

That early encounter fixed my impression of him as a man of uncommon generosity and deep humanity. The memory of it would come to shape my reaction, years later and in America, when bumps developed in my relationship with him.

The day after Achebe had left a message with the secretary at the *Guardian*, I rang the author's American number. I expected to hear that he was on his way to Nigeria.

"There's an important conversation I'd like us to have," Achebe said. "Some of my friends and I are talking about setting up an international magazine in America. I have recommended you as the founding editor. I want you to think about whether you'd be interested in doing it, and then let's talk again in three days."

The invitation was an incredible honor, absolutely unexpected. I was flattered that Achebe offered me an opportunity for such a significant turn in my personal life and professional career. I didn't need three days to think about it. I didn't need hours or even minutes. The answer was a firm and irrevocable yes.

For years, beginning from childhood, I had nursed a fantastical dream about living in the United Kingdom, the United States, or the Soviet Union. In 1988, it was as if, in one audacious move—and thanks to Achebe—America had outmaneuvered its rivals and emerged winner of a fierce three-way race for my affection.

NEVER LOOK AN AMERICAN IN THE EYE

Giving my word to Achebe was rather easy. Yet, my initial exultation about relocating to America quickly wore off, leaving a mixed residue of tense anticipation and anxiety.

I handed in notice of my intention to resign from my post at *African Guardian* and proceeded on a monthlong terminal leave. There was a lot to do to wind up my affairs in Lagos and prepare for the next chapter of my life in the United States. I set about the tasks in earnest. The sheer energy demanded by it all, the running hither and thither, helped reduce—but not stave off—my fretting and agitation.

One of the first things I did was to obtain a Nigerian passport for the first time in my life. I had been warned that the US embassy would deny me a visa if I told the bald truth—that I was going to take up an editor's job in America. I couldn't countenance being turned away, my dream nullified. So when I applied for a visa, I had to fib. I told the young American consular chap who interviewed me that I was going for a conference and then a short visit. I don't remember his follow-up questions or my answers, but I recall the brevity of the encounter. Before I knew it, the young man had stamped a rejection on my passport and pushed it to me.

I was stunned by the appalling finality of the decision.

Everything seemed to stand still for an instant and yet to move at a ferocious velocity. I couldn't utter another word to the man; I was tongue-tied. What was there to say? There were too many people in the cavernous waiting room, other Nigerians waiting for their turn to play the lottery of the American visa. Their eyes stabbed me, or so I felt. In their presence, I could not wheedle, beg, and plead. Even if I did, what good would it do? Nor could I form the words to demand an explanation. Had my interviewer seen through my lie, decided that my dream die? Would it help matters if, contrite, I offered to right the story I had told, to revisit and rewrite the lie about going for a conference?

I realized that, cajole or scold, I could not change a thing, much less the mind of the withholder of a visa. Of the stereotypes I had formed then of every white man, there was this: that once he made a decision, he stuck by it. Let the victim of the decision demonstrate its unjustness; let him importune or flail or weep up a lake of tears; let the decision maker's parents entreat a review; in fact, let his long-deceased ancestors arise from the dead and make an eloquent case for reconsideration—the white man's mind was steely, inflexible, and impermeable.

I have never been able to recall how I made it out of that hall of disenchantment. The memory of my exit has remained a blur. Perhaps I had hurried out, desperate to flee from the dream-aborting encounter. Perhaps I had tarried there, too stubborn or too wounded to move. Perhaps I had left slowly, one leisurely footstep placed in front of the other, in no haste lest the other visa dreamers smell my failure and their eyes peel away my despair layer after layer until the bleeding core of me was laid bare.

For sure, my trip and new life had been upended. How was I to gather and mend the broken shards of this dream? What would I tell friends with whom I had shared farewell drinks? How about my colleagues at the *Guardian*: How was I to explain to them that my dream job in America had slipped from my grasp into oblivion?

How was I to recount the dizzying, devastating punch I had been dealt by a capricious consular officer, a puny man-god with the prerogative to bestow or deny a visa, the power to smother dreams or fertilize them?

My memory of that terrible day returns to vividness only after I had made it out of the hall. Once outside of the embassy, I realized I had broken out in a torrent of sweat. Denied a visa, I knew real agony. Was I going to watch my dream falter and stumble? How was I to countenance this woeful nullification of my trip?

I took my case to Nick Robertson, a likable, gregarious acquaintance who worked for the then United States Information Service (USIS). Nick and I got to know each other rather well because he frequently invited me to the agency's events—talks, receptions for visiting American artists, film screenings, parties. My physical anguish must have made quite an impression on him. As I stuttered and fumbled for words to tell my story, he interrupted me in that zestful, ebullient manner of his. He said, point-blank, he didn't see why I should be denied a visa to the United States. And he offered to write a letter to the consular folks pleading a review of my case.

His intervention worked magic. I was reinvited to the embassy, asked to present my documents, and then instructed to take a seat. A little while later, somebody called my name. I approached a kiosk and was handed back my passport—duly stamped with a visa.

"Have a great time in the United States," the consular official who handled the transaction said. I must have made some grunting sounds, for I was too emotionally edgy to speak.

The day I came out of the embassy, visa finally in hand, it was as if a dead dream had jerked back to life. I could exhale again, with ease, for things were righted, the promise of a new life salvaged.

I set about completing a few tasks in Lagos—shopping, making farewell rounds to friends, informing my landlord of my relocation. Then I traveled to my southeast hometown of Amawbia to spend a week with my parents.

The first time we sat down to talk, my parents remarked on the jumbo salary I was going to earn in America. I was not to become a spendthrift, they cautioned. Instead, I was to cultivate a frugality dictated by an established practice within our extended family. That practice imposed an obligation on members of the family with the financial means to help pay the school fees of those coming behind. It was a formula for lifting up everybody in the wider extended family. In that spirit, my parents said I was to take up responsibility for paying the school fees of my youngest brother, Oguejiofo, and two male cousins, Emeka and Ndubuisi. Once pronounced, the matter was settled; I proudly accepted the responsibility.

My parents must have expected that I would regularly send money to support them. Parents made sacrifices to put their children through schools or into some profession. In return, once established in a job, trade, or profession, children were expected to cater to some of their parents' needs in old age or after retirement. I recognized the sacredness of that obligation. My parents didn't raise it explicitly because they knew that I knew my duty by them; it went without saying.

I could sense that my parents were even tenser than I was about my departure to America. They expressed their foreboding in separate ways, consistent with their respective personalities.

Father tried to mask his nervousness. We'd pass each other and he would tighten his jaws or turn his face slightly away, as if to keep me from reading his emotion, or he would whistle in a way that suggested nonchalant cheeriness. Sometimes, he would look me in the face and attempt to beam, but merely manage a grin. A few times, I surprised him staring at me, wearing a worried look he'd quickly unscramble. Was he wondering if I was up to the challenge Achebe had placed on my shoulder? Or was he seized by a deeper fear, the possibility he'd lose a son—whatever that loss might mean—to America? It was not in his nature to verbalize his fears.

He had fought in World War II in Burma, reaching that turf of war chiefly on a ship. That was the extent of his travels outside of Nigeria. In some profound way, that war defined him. There was something of the stoic soldier in his carriage. His face was ever imperturbable, as if conditioned to mask fear and allied emotions.

Mother did not have Father's flair for stoicism, his mechanism for holding emotions at bay. She had never traveled outside Nigeria's borders. Her worries about my forthcoming trip were raw, urgent, and palpable. They affected me, kept me edgy. Her anxiety took the form of questions that cascaded. What would I do about food? Would I know to eat a balanced diet and make the time to feed myself? What about friends—would I be able to find good ones? How was I to know when to rest, how to get adequate sleep? Would I remember to pray each day, to go to Mass each Sunday? Could I learn enough about American customs to keep out of trouble? What if I found myself in a corner, how could I wriggle out?

I answered each question with a smile, a spree of yeses, and assurances that I would be fine. Yet her questions kept coming, unceasing, all week long.

A day before my return to Lagos, my parents offered a Mass to put me in God's care. That evening, they invited several uncles, aunts, a few other relatives, and some friends to gather at our family home. It was a sumptuous affair, featuring some of my favorite Igbo dishes: *ukwa, akpu na ofe onugbu, ji abubo, agwa na oka, ji oko*. There was also an ample supply of fresh, frothy palm wine, both the sweetish *ngwo* and its more potent, sour sibling, *nkwu*. I savored the meals and drank to my heart's content. Yet, I couldn't suppress the hovering sense of being the center of a mini–Last Supper, a prodigal adventurer about to venture out into the uncertain, unknown, perilous turf of America.

The gathering was also meant to serve as a counseling durbar, an opportunity for each elder to offer me a nugget or two of wisdom and to speak prayers that cleared away any impediments on my path.

The guests included my father's immediate younger brother, Augustine, a trader who went by the praise name of Ochendo (he who provides a shade); my only paternal aunt, Mgbogo, a beautiful, ocher-complexioned woman everybody addressed as Eleti (short for "Electric," a reference to her lightness of skin); and Uncle Linus, an engineer and Father's youngest sibling.

My siblings, cousins, and I revered Uncle Linus. He was as close to a mythic figure as we knew. He was the first member of the Ndibe family to acquire university education, graduating with a second-class upper degree in electrical engineering from the University of Nigeria, Nsukka. And he had even lived and studied for two years in the then West Germany, the first member of the Ndibe family to step foot in Europe. He was a brainy man, and people said he missed earning a first class by a mere sliver. He was the first Ndibe to own a car, a Toyota Corolla. We, the younger Ndibes, were fond of washing the car until its burgundy paint sparkled. When it fell to me to wash the car, I'd often take the driver's seat, start the ignition, and drive it to and fro. If my uncle was nowhere in sight, I'd sometimes steal away in the car, even though I did not have a license. I relished cruising around town. I'd tap at the horn to draw attention to me whenever I caught sight of some girl I wished to impress. Then I'd wave at her, the thrill of being noticed behind the wheel more than compensating for the scolding I would receive from my uncle if he discovered I'd taken his prized vehicle on a jaunt.

We, the Ndibe youngsters, greatly admired Uncle Linus. He'd set academic standards that empowered our own dreams of reaching high, soaring far beyond our parents' accomplishments. He helped pay school fees for my siblings, cousins, and me. As a senior civil servant, in fact the first in our family to crack the middle-class ceiling, he had the means—and the inclination—to buy us the occasional gift that our parents could not afford.

My older brother, John, and I felt greatly pained when our

parents flatly refused to pay a local tailor to make each of us a pair of bell-bottom pants. Such pants were the rage during part of the 1970s. John and I attended numerous parties where we stood out as the only ones who did not sport the wavy, wide-rimmed pants. We detested the dubious distinction. Yet, when we broached the idea of keeping up with our set's sartorial trend, our parents would not hear us out before swatting away the subject.

Traumatized, we took our case to Uncle Linus. We did our best to describe the pain of feeling like fashion oddities in the company of our peers. Somehow, our plaintive accounts of resembling social impostors so moved Uncle that he agreed to intercede with our parents.

With the two of us in tow, he began to talk to our parents. We thought he made an excellent, unimpeachable case. Our parents listened coolly as he spoke, Father's jaws tightened, Mother wringing her hands, as was her wont. Then, once Uncle Linus finished speaking, our mother began to respond. That was a hint of trouble, for our mother was more apt than our father to take a hardline position. She and our father had nothing against us dressing like other youngsters, she assured our uncle. It was just that, as he knew, they didn't have much money; they couldn't afford the luxury of their children following the vicissitudes of fashion. If we wanted books, if we needed anything that would keep us intellectually sharp, they were willing to make sacrifices to get us those. But they would not enable us to chase after every whim of fashion. That, she said, was all there was to say.

As if the finality of that answer weren't disconcerting enough, Uncle Linus, our supposed advocate in chief, became a turncoat. He told our parents that he not only understood their position, he also sympathized with it. He began to lecture my brother and me on fashion, stressing how ephemeral, illusory, and promiscuous it was. Any pleasure we derived from following fashion trends, he warned us, would be fleeting, here now, now gone as gossamer.

I was about to resign to hopelessness when Uncle Linus's tone switched again, his support swung, once more, to our side. He asked our parents' permission to let him pay for a pair of bell-bottom pants for my brother and me. And he was ready to throw in a pair of high-heeled shoes for each of us. Our parents said, in a gentle but visibly disappointed voice, that they would not stand in his way.

John and I got our bell-bottom pants and six-inch shoes. For the first time in a long time, we looked forward to the next big social gathering. I imagined myself waltzing in, pictured smiles all around, eyes pasted on our pants and shoes, in admiration.

A week or two after, my brother and I strode into a party in our new outfits, our moods buoyant. We noticed that something was amiss. Nobody else wore those bell-bottom pants or high-heeled shoes. Instead, the pants were tapered, the shirts much looser than the skin-hugging style that was reigning the last time we looked. The shoes were now stilettoes, heels modest, their pointy tips adorned with flat metal rivets. Nobody had cared to warn us that a new style had come to town, had seized the throne—however momentarily—in the ever-mercurial, fickle world of sartorial taste. Fashion had played its capricious game, sucker punched us where it hurt most, in our very egos. I recall that nobody said a word to us of derision, censure, or pity. It was not a nasty crowd in that way. Besides, many of our male counterparts respected my elder brother, for being something of a math wizard, and me—for my prowess in the English language. But few girls would wish to be seen dancing with boys who were out of fashion. In that sense, we might as well have been hoisted up on a stage, our ridiculously ancient fashion exhibited for all who had a fastidious sense of fashion to behold and mock. Fashion had punished me—just about enough.

That day, I renounced the deity of fashion and all its sneaky, whimsical ways. It was the last time I ever paid heed to any fashion or fad.

At the farewell feast, my parents and other relatives piled me with advice, instructions on what to do, what not do.

"Make sure you don't bring us a white woman for a wife," Auntie Eleti said. Her face bore a mischievous expression, a look that implied I was the sort of rebel to surprise her and other relatives by taking a Caucasian bride. Everybody fixed eyes on me, reading my reaction.

"What have white women ever done to you?" I asked my aunt, laughing.

"Did you hear me say they did anything to me?" she said.

"Don't you think there are good white women?"

"I am sure there are," she answered. "Every people have good and bad women. But we want a wife whose tongue we can understand."

Eleti was the only one of my father's siblings without a scintilla of formal education. She spoke no English, even though—like most Nigerians—she understood a few basic words of the language. I sensed that her stipulation that I not marry a woman with a foreign tongue was not exclusively—or even primarily—about language. Her concern was much deeper: she didn't want me to have a wife who would disdain or reject the bonds of kinship she and other kinsfolk considered sacrosanct.

I promised not to bring home a wife she would not approve of.

"Eheh!" she exclaimed, relieved.

"When you get there, you must be on your guard," Uncle Ochendo chipped in. "And the first thing to remember is this: never look an American in the eye."

My face registered astonishment. As if he anticipated my question, Uncle Ochendo explained.

"Americans can't stand any stranger looking them in the face. They take it as an insult. It's something they don't forgive. And every American carries a gun. If they catch you, a stranger, looking them in the face, they will shoot."

I had never heard about that eye-contact taboo. Yet, I wasn't about to doubt my uncle. I promised not to disregard his counsel.

No immediate relative of mine had ever been to America. Where then did Uncle Ochendo get the impression that Americans abhorred being looked in the face? And so much that they'd shoot anybody who dared?

It was much later—weeks after my arrival in America—that I thought my way to an answer, perhaps *the* answer. In all likelihood, American movies had sown the idea in my uncle's mind.

Years ago, when I was still in secondary school, American movies would be shown once every few months in one pastoral town or another. Wherever they came, the townsfolk—men, women, and youngsters—would gather in an open space, often a soccer field, for a night at the movies. To this day, I have never fathomed— nor have I found anybody who knows—the source of the movies. Perhaps it was the brainchild of the Central Intelligence Agency. It was in the heyday of the Cold War. What better way for the CIA to impress the heck out of us—to win the undecided hearts of Nigerians—than to show us images of the confident, swaggering, swashbuckling American.

The movies were almost always westerns. They were frequently old black-and-white affairs, the screen a broth of blinking lights and flickering lines. There was an invariably odd quality to the audio, often a gap between the movement of the actors' lips and the sound of their words. Add the projector's constant whir, and you'd get a sense of how hard it was to follow the action. I don't remember ever being able to discern what the actors were saying. I'd wager that nobody else did. And perhaps that was all part of the design, that the unintelligibility of the actors' speech should lend a heightened poignancy to their gestures.

The byword was raw action. We watched, enrapt, as the actors rode their horses over some wild, rugged terrain, drove cars across a landscape that seemed, itself, to be whirling past, or congregated in a bar.

In fact, some of the most frenzied moments in the movies took place in bars. Unable to understand the actors' words, I could hardly grasp what their bar brawls were about. It sufficed that, whenever two or more actors gathered in a bar, there was guaranteed to be action. Something about their faces promised a feud, action. A cigarette would hang from each actor's lips. The smoke would rise and curl in the air, then drift away as the actor sipped from a glass of spirits. I recall being fascinated by the actors' eyes, pensive, alert, or serene.

There were always aficionados among the open-air spectators. They were usually older adults who had seen many more of these westerns. As a barroom scene edged toward "action," these buffs would come alive, foretelling the dramatic turn of events. Looking back, they seemed anxious to impress the neophytes among us by predicting what would come next. Sometimes they voiced their predictions in hushed tones, other times rather loudly. One habitué would say, *That man you're looking at,* kai, *he is pure terror! Don't be fooled by his quiet manner. Just wait and see what he'll do.* Another: *Keep your eyes on the bearded one: he's a ferocious shooter!* Yet another: *When you see him gulp down his drink like that, he's ready to start slaughtering people.*

Often, as if cued by the whisperers, an actor would rise and tread his way, slowly, resolutely toward some equally determined, fearless foe in a crowded bar. One actor or two or several would close in, approaching the spot of action. The combatants would stand toe to toe. A thrill would wash over us. Most of us would fall silent, waiting. Only the aficionados could be heard, more animated, predicting the imminence of a blowup, even the outcome of the fiery feud. The actors would exchange words that were—for all we cared—in a coded, esoteric language.

I would be in the grip of anticipation, tightly wound. The actors' verbal exchanges ceased. They went into the stare-down phase, their eyes pepper hot, brows creased, jaws locked, lips sucked in, nostrils twitching. The stare-down signaled the inevitability of a fight. Sometimes it was fisticuffs but more often a gun duel. Once a fight started, the hitherto-silent spectators were swept up into a state of voluble excitement. Hoots and hollers rent the air as bullets flew here and there and everywhere, actors feinting, dashing, diving, ducking. Then the frenzy reached a crescendo as bullets hit bottles, smashing them, splashing the air.

When the cinematic feast was over, we walked home. We felt emptied out from the sheer excitement, the sorrowful parts of our lives momentarily forgotten, our bodies ready for deep sleep, even if for one night. We talked excitedly, adults and youngsters alike, about the actors' swagger, about the fight scenes, about all those bodies that hurtled from atop speeding horses, about the shattered bottles and the splash they made. It was as if we didn't want any of those spectacular images to ever slip away, erased from our awe-struck minds.

If my conjecture is right—that the CIA was behind the movies, that the agency's purpose was to impress us—then I reckon the gambit a grand success. We were duly dazzled. Perhaps the CIA—or whoever sponsored those movies—had stamped in Uncle Ochendo's mind the impression that Americans would not stand for anybody staring them in the face. A mere flicker of eye contact could ignite a hail of bullets, lead to death in a flash.

☆ ☆ ☆
MY COMMISSION AND A CHILLY
AMERICAN RECEPTION

Before my trip to the United States, I visited Chinua Achebe at his home in Nsukka. He had retired after many years of teaching at the University of Nigeria but had kept his official residence. He returned there between intermittent, semester-long stints at a variety of American colleges and universities. He had just come back from a yearlong teaching spell at the University of Massachusetts Amherst. The purpose of my visit was to receive my marching orders. He was the person who had invited me to America, and he was my sponsor in chief.

He and I repaired to a clearing in the small garden behind his home. We found some shade cast by a cluster of low-hanging trees, and sat opposite each other in wooden chairs. Dappled light danced on his face as he sipped tea while I drank from a cold, green bottle of beer.

I was nervous, and the drippy bottle of beer did little to calm me. My agitation had nothing to do with being in Achebe's presence. I had visited his home several times before and had sat with him for long hours, in a spare, neat living room or under the garden's shaded foliage. He always had a calm avuncular air about him. A Nigerian journalist had once observed, aptly, that Achebe's clean-shaven, placid face resembled a cleric's.

It was the weight of my impending assignment in the United States that left me uneasy, a bit shaky. I fixed on Achebe's every gesture. He spoke in Igbo, a choice that somehow rendered the occasion more solemn. As he talked, his hands spliced air, brows furrowed and relaxed, eyes narrowed and widened, like a conductor using non-verbal cues to create emphases. A man averse to wasting words, he spoke hesitantly, as if each syllable of every word had first to be chewed over, rolled in the mouth, and then uttered. Sometimes his voice hardly rose above a whisper as he expressed his vision for the magazine he was handing me the challenge to birth in the United States.

Achebe's manner was, as usual, demure. That fact made his words weighty, pregnant with significance. He spoke in his accustomed circumspect, indirect style, reminiscent of a village elder's deft verbal dance.

He began by explaining how the idea for the magazine originated. It had emerged from a meeting with some Nigerians who attended a party for his last novel, *Anthills of the Savannah*. It had been agreed to set up the magazine outside of Nigeria, a medium to monitor what was happening not just in Nigeria and Africa but also to people of African descent around the world. Achebe said he had proposed me as the right choice for founding editor.

He touched on the approaching 21st century, and the need for Africa and its people to find a path to a dynamic future. He hinted that the coming millennium offered people of African descent a new opportunity to set the agenda for their own renewal and development. He spoke about Nigeria's inevitable role in what one of the continent's greatest nationalist figures, Nnamdi Azikiwe, called "renascent Africa." Yet Nigeria's present was as troubled as its future was uncertain. Nobody could foretell, Achebe said, how Nigeria was going to shape up

Even though he spoke ever so delicately, poking at the subject as if with a snail's horn, the context lent clarity to his statement. He didn't have to spell out what he meant. For me the only question was whether I was up to the task. And I felt ready, even if a tinge of anxiety was present.

ON DECEMBER 10, 1988, less than two weeks after that discussion with Achebe, I left Lagos on a direct Nigeria Airways flight bound for New York's JFK International Airport. It was a bumpy experience, approximately eleven hours, the longest time, then, I had ever been airborne. It was also my first trip outside of Africa.

My nerves were shot to pieces. Much of it had to do with the turbulence. A virgin in transcontinental air travel, I translated each shiver of the aircraft as a calamity about to happen. My fear was compounded by the seemingly endless, dark, and bottomless waters of the Atlantic Ocean below. I was also a non-swimmer who could sweep gold for the fastest time to the bottom of any pool.

I imagined the ocean seethed that particular day, sinister and grumpy. I couldn't expunge from my mind the idea that some mysterious force, kin to the monsters of the Bermuda Triangle, could suck the plane clean from the night sky and into all that implacable, churning waste. Silently I resolved that, if I made it alive to America, I would stay put. I would never risk that dreadful passage all over again. Never.

My uncle had warned me against looking Americans in the eye but he had not prepared me for winter, the rudest, most savage challenge I would face in America.

After a long, nerve-shattering flight, the Nigeria Airways plane began its unhurried descent to JFK International Airport on December 10, 1988. It was a sunny, cloudless day. Through the aircraft's window, I looked down, half in awe, half in dread, at huddles of skyscrapers, a crisscross of bridges over a shimmering expanse of water, a maze of streets and highways that carved up and contained New York City's sprawl. Then the aircraft's tires met the tarmac.

I felt a swell of relief. The flying beast roared and rattled as it bar-
reled forward and then cut off the chase. I couldn't believe it; I was
in America. Finally, one of my dreams as a youngster was realized.

The long, winding line to the immigration desk moved too
slowly for my comfort, but there was nothing to do but wait. I
clenched and unclenched my fists to keep calm.

Then, suddenly, I stood in front of an immigration officer. He
held up my passport and peered at the photo. Then, as he looked
in my face, I quickly fixed my gaze on the flat plane of the cubicle.

"You're here on business. What business exactly?" he asked.

"To attend a conference," I said, scrupulously avoiding eye
contact.

"And how long is the conference?"

"One week."

"Do you have any other plans?"

"No."

He stamped my passport and held it out to me. After picking
up my lone, small suitcase—I had packed light, on purpose—I
stopped at the customs station. Tucked away in my suitcase were
two or three bags made from crocodile skin. A cousin of mine, who
lived at the time in Weymouth, Massachusetts, had advised that
I bring them. He could find me buyers who would pay several
times the amount I spent on the bags. A hard-faced customs officer
unzipped my suitcase and pulled out the bags.

"You're not allowed to bring these in," he said in a flat, censorious tone. He tossed the bags aside, rezipped my suitcase, and
waved me on.

I had a sinking feeling, the more intense because I felt powerless to argue. But I was determined to conjure a lively spirit. I set
for the exit sign, a willful bounce to my gait. Chinua Achebe had
arranged for Chudi Uwazurike, a Harvard-educated Nigerian soci-
ologist at City College, to meet me. The man would be waiting at
the arrival lounge, Achebe had told me. It would be easy to find

him, Achebe added, as he would be holding up a piece of paper with my name scribbled on it.

My name on a piece of paper! The idea struck me as grand and charming, as if I were being inducted into the roll of the famous.

Achebe hadn't warned me of the sight and buzz of a *humanhive*. Dozens of people held up papers or small boards in the bustling promenade, the names of arriving passengers typed or scrawled on them. Twice I walked the length of the aisle, looked in vain for my name. Then it dawned on me: perhaps Uwazurike was supposed to pick me up outside the arrival hall, not inside.

The exit doors parted as I approached, and I pushed my cart outside. I knew, instantly, that I had erred terribly; I had walked, willy-nilly, into an air ambush. I felt surrounded, stormed by a swirling gust of arctic air. The sting of it forced me to halt. Here I was, a lifelong tropical being, buffeted by air so frigid it seemed to drill its way to my marrow. Nothing in the vocabulary of my experience prepared me for this assault.

I pirouetted, faced the arrival lounge. Thankfully the doors parted again, to let me back in. I pushed the cart to an empty seat and plunked down. As I sat there, mystified, I looked around me, watched people. A ceaseless procession of people walked in, walked out of the lounge. Everybody else wore winter gear, complete with caps, hoods, mufflers, and gloves. To me, in a light cotton shirt underneath a sport coat, the others were padded up. Their world, from all appearances, still had its center, life its familiar rhythms. My own center had disappeared. I was marooned in an unspeakably cold place. My agitated mind churned with questions that had no calming answers. What could have happened to Uwazurike? I knew that many Nigerians had an elastic sense of time, hence the phrase "Nigerian time." It meant that an appointment that was set, say, at 1 P.M. could take place anytime from then till 6 P.M. Was Uwazurike one of those adherents to Nigerian time? If so, how many hours would I wait before he showed up? Once he came, how would he and I recognize each other? There were lots and lots of people in the airport lounge, travelers and their escorts and goodness knows who else. Achebe had not given me a physical description of Uwazurike, and I doubt I had been described to him.

A worse scenario: What if Uwazurike had forgotten about me altogether, or had had to make a last-minute trip out of the city? What if he never showed up?

I had two telephone numbers on me. One was for a cousin who lived somewhere in Massachusetts, the other for Bart Nnaji. If the day wore on and my host didn't show up, I was going to call my cousin or Nnaji. Yet, this thought brought me little comfort. I didn't know how to use the pay phone. It was worse: I didn't even have any US currency to use to make a call.

With time, a heaviness began to press itself on my eyelids. My body, leaden, slowly slipped toward sleep. I began to tap my shoes on the floor, a desperado's effort to shake off sleep. It was a tough battle. I was afloat in a half-conscious, half-asleep state. Everybody else seemed grotesquely inflated and alien-like, mini-astronauts dressed for space. How long was I in that state, slipping and rising, embroiled in a feud between weary body and desperate will? How long did I try to fend off that creeping power that, seizing limb after limb, deadened me?

"Are you Okey?"

The words smashed into my woozy consciousness. It had come from my left flank, the voice. A light-skinned man had his eyes trained on me.

"Are you Okey?" he asked again.

I affirmed with a nod.

"Professor Chudi Uwazurike," he said. He offered his right hand. I extended mine for the handshake, his grip American-firm. "Have you been waiting for long?"

"About an hour," I said. It had certainly been longer; in fact, had seemed like days.

"So sorry. I had a class. And then I was trapped in traffic. Very heavy traffic."

I was too relieved to mind his lateness.

"Let's go," he said. That instant, he paused and gave me a sharp, quizzical look. His perplexed expression was that of a man who'd suddenly discovered something odd, if not grotesque, about my person. "Where's your jacket?" he asked.

I pointed to sport jacket I was wearing.

"No, I mean your winter jacket," he clarified.

Winter jacket? *Winter* jacket? I shrugged.

"Wow, *this* is all you brought?" He shook his head, gesturing at the jacket. A look of disbelief, a suggestion of alarm, seized his face.

Why, nobody had warned me to gird against this foe called winter. Did Uwazurike's expression mean that winter had laid ambush for me, ready to pounce the moment I stepped outside?

"You have arrived on a very cold day," he volunteered.

The information stung. In fact, I took it personally. America had chosen to be chilly, frost mannered. It had flung its harsh arctic air at me.

I was not altogether ignorant about winter. Or, to be more specific, I was not new to the word. Back in Nigeria, I had gone through a phase when I read lots of American writers—Richard Wright, Ralph Ellison, John Steinbeck, James Baldwin, Langston Hughes, William Faulkner. I was also quite fond of *Time* and *Newsweek* magazines, copies of which I sometimes bought from street vendors. The Lagos Island office of the United States Information Service stocked a variety of American newspapers, magazines, and books. I used to frequent USIS for one event or another, to see some of their friendly staff or to borrow books. As a roaming reader, I had encountered the word "winter" in numerous books, on numerous occasions. But I never lingered on the word, I never dwelled on it, nor did I ever pause to really, deeply, *experience* it.

I had always thought that winter was the American version of what the Igbo call *ugulu,* otherwise more widely known across West Africa as harmattan. Harmattan is a dry cold wind that emanates from the Sahara Desert and sweeps through much of West Africa from the latter part of the -ember months through to March.

Growing up in Nigeria, I had witnessed many harmattan seasons. The harmattan brings fine granules of dust that cause coughs, redden the eye, color the skin ashy, and lend the atmosphere a patina of grey. It also gives the air a tinge—a mere tinge—of cold. At the height of the harmattan season, the temperature drops in the mornings, hovering around fifty-five degrees Fahrenheit. In tropical Nigeria, that's what we call cold.

Whenever I had come across the word "winter" in print, I mentally transposed "harmattan" in its place. Why would I pack a special winter jacket for my trip to New York City when my people had never needed to invent a harmattan jacket? The entire arsenal of our combat against *ugulu*-grade cold consisted of Vaseline (to sheen up dry, scaly skin), a sweater (usually worn by the very elderly and children), a handkerchief (to ward off dust), and a pair of sunglasses (to protect the eyes from airborne sand).

Harmattan pretty much left you alone, unless you provoked it. And the gravest act of provocation was to take a cold bath or shower early in the morning. The body and cold water were at war during harmattan. The touch of cold water on the skin made you wince, whistle, whoop, and jump. If you knew what was good for you, you warmed your water before bathing.

"You have to wear this," Uwazurike said. He pulled off and handed me his padded winter jacket, hooded, fleece lined, down filled. I wore it, complete with the hood. I suppressed a laugh— amused by how closely I resembled a space-bound astronaut.

We dashed through the parking lot to his car. The instant he started the engine, a steady whoosh filled the car. It was, I realized with astonishment, the rush of heated air. What a novelty, I thought. In Nigeria, all but the poorest car owners had air-conditioning installed in their vehicles.

I brooded while my host drove through the light-suffused night. Taking in the scenes that whirled past, I had the sensation that we were headed into the vast violent belly of a strange implacable city.

My chest was tautly wound, leaden. I felt a sharp sense of loss and danger. The pilgrim's plaintive prayer rose in my mind: *Home, sweet home; there's no place like home.* I had read somewhere that President John F. Kennedy, following a particularly difficult summit with his Soviet rival, Nikita Khrushchev, had declaimed, "It's going to be a long cold winter," or words to that effect. Suddenly, I understood the archaic anxiety contained in that phrase. I had stepped from my warm natal home into the friendless frigidity of an alien land.

After the ordeal at the airport, Uwazurike's home felt cozy and warm. It struck me that its elegance did not depend on lavishness of space but on the tastefulness of its interior, the congruence between space and utility. In it, I experienced another first. Back in Nigeria, people of means almost always owned air-conditioned homes or apartments. And yet here I was in my host's apartment, heat wafting out of every vent.

In my first letters to friends and relatives in Nigeria, I strained to find the language to convey what winter felt like. No, *ugulu*, the harmattan, couldn't stand near—much less beside—winter. In the end, I figured out the only comparison they could relate to: *Winter,* I wrote, *was akin to living inside a refrigerator.*

SLEEPLESS IN NEW YORK

My first night in the United States brought little respite. I had endured eleven hours aboard a Nigeria Airways flight, confined in a tight seat, wedged uncomfortably between two other passengers, one a middle-aged man with a beer belly who snored as a gorilla might, the other a young woman who stayed awake for most of the trip, a curious sneer fixed on her face, as if she were at war with the world in general for subjecting her to the plight of flying economy.

By the time the plane touched down in New York, my body had had enough of the ordeal. I felt ravaged. I sorely needed rest, but sleep was hard to come by.

Uwazurike's wife had greeted me warmly as I walked into their house, a step behind her husband. Moments later, Chudi Uwazurike showed me to a guest room. Folded neatly and placed at the foot of the bed were a towel and a washcloth, a bar of soap resting on top of them.

Their sight reminded me of a practice I had learned from my parents. Whenever a visitor arrived to stay at our home, my parents would ask one of my siblings or me to hoist a bucket of water to the outdoor bathroom. Then they would invite the visitor to go and "wash off the journey." My parents observed the same rite of ablution. On returning from any trip, they'd say, in a tone of urgency, "Let me wash off the journey." As a youngster, I had been intrigued by that habit. It fixed in my mind the idea of a journey as wearying, an exercise in the accumulation of grime, soot, and sweat. A bath revitalized travelers' limbs, cleansed their pores, and rejuvenated their spirits.

As if he read my mind, Uwazurike asked if I wished to take a bath right away.

My hosts' bathroom was so clean you could eat in it. Its air had a hint of scent. For sure, some wealthy people back in Nigeria also had such pristine bathrooms, but I had never been in one. For me, then, the bathroom seemed an advertisement of America's power, prosperity—and excess. There were numerous bars of soap in it, different shapes, sizes, and fragrances. Which one to use? I palmed each one, relished its solidity, held it against my nose, and breathed in. I could not decide. Not to worry, I used two or three. There were also several bottles of shampoo and conditioners. I lathered my hair with each. The showerhead gushed a jet of warm water. The shower soothed me, washed away my weariness. I overstayed in the bathroom, delighted to bask in American excess.

Thereafter, Uwazurike's wife treated me to a delicious Nigerian-style dinner of stewed chicken and rice. It was a perfect first supper in America. And I washed down the food with a glass or two of orange juice, the first time I ever savored the sweet, pulpy drink.

After dinner, we watched TV on a huge screen. Uwazurike flicked from one channel to another, news, sports, a movie. I had never seen TV like this, what seemed like an inexhaustible parade of channels, a bottomless variety. I was amazed by the largeness of the screen and the remote control in Uwazurike's grasp that seemed to conjure up this or that program. Like the soaps and shampoos, the sheer multitude of TV channels was a proclamation both of America's spoiled-rotten prosperity and robust diversity and freedom. It all left me both in awe and dismayed. When Uwazurike invited me to choose what I wished to watch, I felt a slight panic attack. Politely, I declined my host's invitation. Any channel he chose would serve me, I said.

During advert interludes, Uwazurike brought up one issue or another about Nigeria. I found out he was a passionate political pontificator, and he knew and even schmoozed with some of Nigeria's biggest political players. His anecdotes and insights intrigued me. I relished the manner of his enunciation, his air of professorial certitude.

At last, my hosts said I must be jet-lagged. Being my first intercontinental trip, I had no familiarity with what being jet-lagged entailed. I felt fatigued, my body somewhat out of sync, but I didn't feel sleepy. Rather, my mind was alert, agitated. I could not quite articulate what I had expected America to look and feel like, but the America I had seen in my first few hours was somewhat stranger, more mystifying than what I had imagined. Could I ever establish harmony with this America? Could I make peace, ever, with the frosty monster called winter? Would I ever get used to the sheer vastness and spectacle of the American terrain? With America's dizzying parade of material objects? And with that frenetic, no-pause, hurry-on, don't-give-a-damn-about-you stride with which Americans—at least the ones I saw in New York—walked?

Were the Uwazurikes old friends, I would have implored them to tarry with me for a while longer, urged them to keep vigil with me another hour or two. But their tone suggested finality. They had stayed up way past their turn-in time. In referring to my being jet-lagged, they were in fact telling me, the best way they knew, that they were tired. I had to, as the Igbo people say, use my tongue to count my teeth. My hosts had been generous, and they were due their rest. They deserved their sleep, needed their bodies refurbished to take on the challenges of another fast-paced, grueling American day.

I rose, thanked them again for the trouble of picking me up and for the meal. I said my good nights and shambled off to the guest bedroom. The room was warm, the bed comfortable. I sneaked under the soft, padded bedsheet, legs pulled up, as if I aimed that my chin and knees touch. It was the fetal pose of a man cowering in a corner, terrified of some vicious monster.

Finally alone, ensconced in bed, I could not keep my mind from its wandering. I looked in vain for that ecstasy of arrival, all but wiped away by that first savage brush with winter. My body, as though touched anew by frozen fingers, shook violently.

I was always a sound sleeper. In fact, I'd been known to plunk down on a couch in a room filled with exuberant dancers and blaring music, and nod off. My first night in America, I yearned for that facility to slip, easy, into sleep. I wished I could float away to forgetfulness, transported to a state where warmth—or a dream of it—was possible.

Yet, on a day I most desperately pined for sleep, it eluded me. I rolled about in bed, my mind a magnet, drawing all manner of disquieting thoughts to itself. I was on edge, close to hypersensitive. The sounds of cars zooming past, of humans talking, breached the walls, vexed my ears. I strained for the awful sound of guns exploding. Luckily, it never materialized.

With sleep not an option, I wished that time would hasten, dawn arrive in a hurry. But time, hope, and terror of the adventurer, was heedless. All night long, I remained restless, trapped between periods of weary wakefulness and fitful sleep.

At last, after hours of unsettling aloneness, I felt Uwazurike's house began to awaken, to stir again. Doors opened and shut, made sharp whiny sounds. I picked up the patter of footsteps, the sucking sound of flushed toilets, the gurgle of water jetting from faucets. The sounds were sweet music. The clink of plates, pots, cutlery, comforted me. There was the sizzle and hiss of food being fried on the stove. Soon, the aroma of fried onions, tomatoes, eggs, and plantains flooded my room. My mouth watered. Yet, I lay in bed, listless and torn. A part of me desired food; another part hoped, with a tinge of desperation, for a final dash of sleep.

I hovered in a daydream state. Curled up to ward off the hint of cold that had come with the morning, I tried to identify the sounds and smells that intruded on me.

A light knock on the door snapped me out of languor. "Yes, come in," I answered.

"Are you awake?" It was Chudi Uwazurike's baritone voice.

I wasn't sleeping, but "awake" wasn't a word that quite defined my state, either. Still I said, "Yes."

"Breakfast is almost ready," he announced.

In the bathroom I brushed my teeth. Then I took another shower, ablution to prepare me for my second day in America. It was a shorter shower time than the night before, but I repeated the nighttime routine of lathering my body with the different soaps, washing my hair with several shampoos and conditioners. One day in America, and I already relished excess, savored variety.

After breakfast, I bid goodbye to Uwazurike's family. Then he took me via the subway to New York's cavernous Port Authority Bus Terminal. The descent down a flight of stairs to the subway platform was a novel experience, at once terrifying and exciting. I felt like a burrowing being surrounded by many other such creatures. Down on the platform, I had the sensation of being cast into a Homeric cauldron. Hundreds—perhaps thousands—of people milled about. Their faces seemed staunchly closed and mute. Every space appeared occupied, but there was the impression that each man, each woman, stood alone, apart. In the cavern, the sound of trains pulling in, pulling out, was a horrendous belch. A horde of passengers would emerge from the belly of each train and others would rush in to take the vacated spaces. The train would pull away, its sound like a metallic monster's hideous roar. Uwazurike nudged me into one of the cars. All the seats were taken. He instructed me to grab a horizontal bar. I had yet to secure a grip before the train sped off. Thrust forward, I barged into a tall man. "I'm sorry," I said quickly, too embarrassed and scared to look at him. He said nothing; I had the impression he glowered at me.

I was still ill at ease when we arrived at the Port Authority Bus Terminal. Here, I felt even more swamped—by people, by human and mechanical sounds. The dashing bazaar of people made me afraid I could crash into somebody or lose Uwazurike. He bought me a ticket and waited until I boarded the Peter Pan bus bound for Springfield, Massachusetts. The bus trip was about three hours, with several stops. In my angst-ridden state, the journey seemed to stretch for an eternity.

Much to my relief, Bart Nnaji was at the bus station in Springfield to welcome me. We drove in his Saab sedan to his home in Florence, a wooded suburb next to Northampton. I joined his family to eat a meal of curry chicken and white rice. His wife offered me some take-away chicken in a large plastic container with a cover.

Afterward, Nnaji drove me to 38 North Prospect Street in Amherst, my first residential address in America. Built in 1892, the house was a rather grand Victorian-style home, with a TV room, a dining room, a living room, a large kitchen, three bathrooms, and three bedrooms. Chinua Achebe and his family had lived there for a month or so during the tail end of his visiting professorship at the University of Massachusetts Amherst.

Nnaji left after showing me through the house. Once alone, I realized that the grandeur and commodiousness of my new residence unnerved me, as if I had been moved into a haunted gothic home and left severely alone.

I couldn't free my mind from my uncle's dire warning—that every American owned and carried a gun. It didn't help that it was the dead of winter. By 5 P.M., darkness had fallen outside, wreathed the house. I couldn't see beyond the front door. Yet, I knew that anybody outside could peer at me through the front door or the home's large windows.

Some gunman, I feared, might be prowling in the dark, in absolute anonymity, scouting me out. The fear exasperated me, but I felt powerless to dispel it. It recalled a fear that seized and menaced me as a young schoolchild.

We lived then in Enugwu Ukwu, a town of several hundred thousand people in southeastern Nigeria. My father was the town's postmaster, my mother the headmistress of one of its two elementary schools. The buzziest part of the town was its marketplace, located on one part of a busy tarred road. Some days, I would steal away from my parents' watchful eyes and head for the market. I could always count on meeting some of my school friends. We loved to gather at the edge of the market. We would kick around soccer balls. We would take in the sights and sounds of traffic, traders, and buyers. We would daydream. And we would talk about any subject that caught our fancy.

Across from the market, on the other side of the tarred road, was a cemetery. It was nondescript, this cemetery, except for a huge marbled tomb that was ringed round with steel chains. One day, as we dawdled near the marketplace, one of us pointed across the road at the cemetery.

"Does anybody know why that tomb is chained?" he asked.

None of us had any idea.

"I will tell you," he said.

According to him, the occupant of the tomb had been a notorious member of a secret cult. The cult had given him a choice between (a) enjoying a long life with modest means and (b) acquiring spectacular wealth but dying at a relatively young age. The man had chosen option B and had undergone the requisite diabolical ritual to seal the pact.

Yet, when death came calling, the man had turned bitter. He'd become a bullying fiend-ghost. Some nights, he would arise from the grave, adorn his glittering attire, and plant himself by the roadside. Any foolhardy pedestrian who happened to pass the cemetery after dark faced merciless beating by the ghost. Other nights, the man jaunted to his home. There, he'd punish his sleeping wife and children with vicious punches until neighbors ran to the scene, alarmed by the shrieks and screams. It took the services of a powerful *dibia,* a traditional healer and the closest thing to a priest, to restrain the unruly ghost. It was this *dibia* who ordered that a steel fence be built around the tomb, to finally contain, cordon off, the pestering ghost.

For months after hearing this story, I was certain that the ghost would breach the steel barricade—and that, for sure, he would come after me. Night after night, I would lie on a mat, wide awake, in a room with my siblings, unable to fall asleep. For a long time, my eyes would scour the darkness, filled with hideous, haunting shapes and images. And then, thoroughly exhausted, I'd succumb to sleep.

This childhood fear was similar to the fear I felt my second night in America, my first in Amherst. I had conjured up an armed, faceless foe I was now unable to dismantle, unmake. I had allowed myself to imagine that this invisible enemy was set to do me in, and in a final, decisive way. What—who—could prevent this foe from taking deadly aim at me, pulling the trigger?

I felt trapped, hemmed in inside my new, well-lit abode. I proceeded to pull shut all the blinds. Then I turned off all the lights in the house save for a table lamp in the TV room.

I flipped on the TV and found a movie. I sat on a couch and gazed at the television. It was an absentminded sort of gaze. I was less interested in the movie than in using the TV to lure my mind away from this aching idea that some armed, sinister bully was out *there*. The movie could not transport me. That, or I just was unable to shake off the notion that some armed predator prowled outside.

It dawned on me: my second night in America was shaping up to be even more tormented than the first. I had never slept in a house, of any shape or size, all by myself, much less lived alone. In fact, my last apartment in Lagos was something of a mecca, always abuzz with relatives, friends, or colleagues who would stay for anything between a few hours and several months.

In Nigeria, houses were built either with concrete or mud, not the wood that many Americans favored. The wooden floor at 38 North Prospect creaked. I tried treading stealthily, like an artful burglar doing his best not to awaken his victims. Still the creaking stayed constant. Pressed to pee, I groped my way to the nearest bathroom, tried to hold my breath. Even then, the creaking taunted me.

Hours passed, but I remained awake, afraid. In fact, my fear fed sleeplessness. It was well past 2 A.M. when I decided to turn off the TV and head upstairs. I tiptoed up the staircase and into the master bedroom. I flicked on the light, revealing a huge, antique bed, waiting for me. The curlicues in the bed's wooden frame lent it an air of ancientness.

For a few minutes, I debated what to do with the bedroom light. A part of me wanted to leave it on through the night. But what if a sniper hoisted himself up on a ladder, snooped at me as I slept? I turned it off. Instantly, a thick darkness swallowed me. Unnerved, I quietly lowered myself on the bed. I curled up and then gingerly pulled the covers over my body.

I didn't expect to tumble off into deep sleep, and I didn't. Supine, I moped at the parade of ghostly faces in the layered, liquid darkness. From outside came the ceaseless chorus of insects and other creatures. Now and again, the house itself would seem to sputter or groan, as if some disembodied presences had sneaked into the space to keep me company, torment me.

I WAS SURPRISED WHEN the phone by my bedside began to ring. I groped about, picked it up, and croaked, "Hello."

"Okey, Professor Nnaji here. Did I wake you up?"

"It's okay," I said.

And it truly was. My body had defied fear, triumphed over nocturnal nightmares, and surrendered to sleep. My second night in America, first night in Amherst, I had found a way—*hurrah, hurrah*—to rest.

"Do you need anything?" Nnaji asked.

I knew he couldn't give me what I was desperate for: some human company. Would he even relate if I voiced that earnest wish?

"No, nothing," I said.

NIGERIAN, GOING DUTCH

On December 14, 1988, I went to see Nnaji at his office at the University of Massachusetts Amherst. He'd invited me over to talk to Karen U, a tall, wiry African American woman who wore a military-low haircut, her vein-lined arms an exhibit of sinewy, defined muscles.

After introducing Karen to me, Nnaji told her I was a major Nigerian journalist who had just arrived in the United States to take up editorship of a new magazine. Nnaji then addressed me.

He said Karen had sought him out for advice about a trip she contemplated making to Nigeria. Since I had arrived from Nigeria only days ago, he felt that my insights would better serve Karen.

Karen took it from there.

From her first moments of awakening awareness as a child, she had wanted to know who her father was and the origin of her last name, which was rather unusual among her peers' surnames. She had asked the only person she felt should know, her mother. But for years, her mother had balked against discussing her paternity. And then the woman was diagnosed with cancer.

As the disease ravaged her, Karen's mother finally relented. She gave to her daughter the information she had withheld for years.

In sum, the dying woman told her daughter that, in the late

1950s, she had fallen in love—or merely fallen in—with a Nigerian man who was then a graduate student at Fordham University in New York City. As their relationship progressed, she had become pregnant. Meanwhile, the Nigerian had completed his studies. He arranged a trip to Nigeria. He would soon return, he told her. When he did—she never doubted that his word was good—she expected that their relationship would blossom, perhaps into matrimony.

As it turned out, the man never returned to the States. At any rate, he never came back to her. Embittered about being betrayed and jilted, she nevertheless gave birth to her daughter, whom she raised alone. Her resentment took the form of silence, came in her refusal to divulge the identity of her jilter, much less to name him. The only thing that shook that resentful silence, the only thing that could, was the visitation of a horrific disease that wreaked havoc on her body, lent each remaining moment an air of urgency.

One day, just before her struggle against cancer ended in her death, Karen's mother summoned her daughter. "Your father's name is Emmanuel U," the woman said. And then, sticking to the bare bones, she gave her daughter a sketch of what had transpired between the Nigerian and herself.

After burying and mourning her mother, Karen felt a tug deep in her heart. Everything within her, fueled perhaps by the pangs of bereavement, pointed her emotional compass in the direction of Nigeria. Daily, the quest to find her father, to go to his country, grew. It became a consuming desire. It was this hunger that had brought her to Nnaji. And then Nnaji had pointed her in my direction.

Karen's story, told at a feverish pace with intermittent interjections by Nnaji, rent my heart. There were times when the torrent of her words seemed choked off by emotion, the narrative lurching, threatening to fall to pieces or incoherence. At such moments, Nnaji, who had heard the story at least once before, would jump in, throw her a tidbit she had earlier shared with him. Karen would give a quick nod and a nervous smile. Then she would steady her voice, snatch back and stitch up the story—and determinedly continue.

Her pain was all too evident. But there was also in her countenance something even more stubbornly visible, even harder to disguise. It was a quality of hope, a stalwart confidence in the success of her mission to find and unite with her father. I found her pain devastating. But even more heartbreaking was that expression on her face, barely contained, of expectancy and hope. She exuded an exultant sense of anticipation.

I don't know this for sure, but I suspect that Karen's search for her father had an enchanted, if illusory, dimension to it. Earlier in 1988, the movie *Coming to America* had come out and become a commercial hit. Perhaps Karen fantasized about making a triumphant entry into her own mythic kingdom of Zamunda. Perhaps she pictured herself an unheralded princess sashaying in from the shadows, three decades later, her stunned subjects heady with adulation, joyful tears in her eyes, a baby tiara on her head.

Eddie Murphy's movie aside, the late 1980s also teemed with a certain brand of "Africanist" scholars. These scholars turned skin color—pigmentation—into a (perhaps *the*) central paradigm of human experience, of history. Historical and literary texts had opened my eyes to the nature and tragic dimensions of Europe's exploitation of Africa, including the horrific cost of the capture and enslavement of millions of Africans. I knew that Europe's imperial adventurism and its depredation of Africa's human and natural resources had left lasting scars on the African continent and people of African descent. But I was taken aback to hear or read scholars who purveyed a simple, uninflected idea of Europeans as irredeemably nefarious, Africans as unblemished lords, princes, and princesses, preternaturally disposed to nobility. At packed lecture halls, churches, and mosques, the most demagogical of these scholars cast Caucasians as congenitally ice hearted, profit obsessed, resentful of the sun-warmed exaltedness of their dark-skinned brethren. They theorized that Europeans, driven by envy and hunger for gruel, had battered Africa and upset its millennia of splendor.

That perfumed version of African history was very much in the air, indeed reigned, in some circles in late-1980s America. I had a hunch that Karen, in addition to curiosity about her father, also wanted to encounter this blissful Africa.

Karen's story, her plight, reminded me of the biblical narrative of the prodigal son. With two obvious differences: the prodigal was a father who had wandered away from an expectant lover, turned his back on a baby bulging in the womb, and the child in Karen's narrative was a daughter, not a son. And it was not the case that this prodigal father had come looking for his daughter. No, it was the daughter, as in the fable, prepared to cross seven hills and ford seven rivers. It was the daughter, ready to beseech or beguile mischievous or sinister monsters bent on blocking her path, to find her absentee father.

I immediately saw impediments to Karen's looming wanderlust. I knew enough to realize it would not be easy for a voyager to land in Nigeria, a country of more than a hundred million people, and find her way, by asking questions, to the door of a man she had never met before. I knew Nigerians to be famously suspicious of strangers with loads of questions. Few Nigerians would open up readily to such a quester, especially one whose mission, once revealed, would raise social alarms and awaken cultural taboos.

I could tell—from his name—that the man who had fathered Karen was Igbo, like Nnaji and me. The Igbo frowned on the idea of leaving one's child, the creature of one's blood, in the "wild," outside of one's hearth. To be implicated in the abandonment of one's progeny was in the Igbo imagination close to the gravest acts of betrayal. If Karen materialized in Nigeria, unheralded, and announced herself as an abandoned child, the cost of such revelation could prove quite dear—too dear, in fact—for her absentee father. The man would have built other lives, other relationships, other memories and histories apart from the pregnant woman he'd left behind in America, the daughter he'd never ever known much less held in his arms. The sudden, unanticipated appearance of the unknown daughter would unsettle any delicate balance the man had constructed, give a violent jolt to his world.

When she was done telling her story, Karen turned to me. Her silence conveyed all the eloquence of her inquisitiveness. What was she to do next? Was hers a fool's errand, bound to futility? What course was she to take in order to realize her cause? The wordless torrent of her questions, transmitted by something quizzical in her demeanor, frightened me. It was as if she considered me a deep-seeing mystic, a sage, an avatar. I was under pressure to come up with answers, and to do so fast.

I had a lucky spark of inspiration.

"You don't have to travel all the way to Nigeria to find your father," I said.

She gave me a sharp, inquisitive look.

I didn't want to tell her about Nigerians' idiosyncrasies, the likelihood a "foreign" woman inquiring about a man would raise all kinds of suspicion, trigger silence, even deliberately misleading information. I just didn't have the right codes to convey that information, nor was I sure she'd know how to absorb, digest it.

"I think I can find out about your father," I said. It was hard, a strain, to utter the words "your father." In normal circumstances, the words would be uncomplicated, would evoke filial bonds. But not in this circumstance: the woman before me nearly thirty without ever having met the man who fathered her. She hadn't seen a single photo of him, didn't have the faintest idea how he looked. She could walk past him on a street, busy or abandoned, and yet have no inkling his blood flowed in her veins. The only way she could imagine how he looked was to stand before a mirror, look hard at herself, and let her mind wander and wonder, conjure him in her own image.

"How?" she asked.

"I'll use one or two newspapers."

Karen was enrapt as I laid it all out for her.

First, I explained my premise. I was certain that a man who was a graduate student at Fordham in the late 1950s would have achieved significant social status on his return to Nigeria. Lots of people would know him.

I would ask one of my best friends, C. Don Adinuba, to write a short note that would be published on the letters page of the Nigerian *Guardian* newspaper. The note would simply state that C. Don had a message for Emmanuel U, a graduate of Fordham University. It would add a request that anybody who knew Emmanuel U should write to C. Don with the man's address. If Karen's father reached out to C. Don himself, he would be told that an American woman, apparently his daughter, was looking for him. If C. Don got the contact from somebody else, he would pass the information to Karen through me.

Nnaji instantly liked my plan. Karen seemed intrigued, but in no hurry to endorse it. She asked question after question. I gave short or long, sinuous answers, depending on the question. Nnaji said he had to run off to a meeting.

"Have you eaten lunch?" Karen asked me. She was clearly reluctant to end the discussion.

"No."

"Why don't we go to lunch," she proposed.

I smiled to indicate my eagerness. I had been in America for four days, and I was meeting my first generous American.

Let me insert a note of cultural information. In Nigeria, when somebody invites another—or even others—to a meal, it is understood that the inviter will pick up the tab. However, it is unusual for a Nigerian woman to treat a man to a meal in a restaurant. For that matter, it is not common practice for a Nigerian woman to buy a man much of anything. This reality flashed through my mind the moment Karen invited me to go out to lunch. I thought, Well, she's an American woman. And American women are supposed to be "liberated."

We walked a short distance from Nnaji's office, to a restaurant at the University of Massachusetts Campus Center. Karen and I ordered sandwiches, soup, and a soda each. Karen settled down to eating, but I could hardly bite into my food. The reason was her stream of questions. As I talked, she ate. Once I paused to take a bite, she would ask another question—and then get me going.

At a point the questions began to tax my patience. I considered making up a story about another engagement, and running off. But a part of me annulled the scheme. This woman was kind, she had done for me what few Nigerian women had ever done—buy me a meal. I coaxed myself into staying put, paying her back for her grace and generosity with patient attention to her questions.

The waitress came round to ask if we wanted to order anything else. We both said no. A moment later, the waitress leaned in between us and left a bill. She placed the tab equidistant between Karen and me, as if she didn't wish for either of us to have an unfair advantage snatching it up.

I hardly glanced at the bill. Karen had invited me to eat, and I had fulfilled my obligation. Paying for the food and drinks had nothing to do with me.

"We have to go," Karen announced, pulling out her purse and simultaneously motioning toward the bill.

I had long wanted to rise and leave, so I was quick in agreeing it was time to go. But why, I wondered, had Karen pointed to the bill? I thought, Since America has weather as strange as winter, perhaps its people have even stranger customs. Perhaps, before an American pays for your meal, they want you to see how much they

are paying. I made a point of gazing at the bill. Then, looking up
in Karen's direction, I said, "Thank you."

She ignored me, even asked one or two other questions. Then
she said, more emphatically, "We gotta go."

I nodded my agreement.

She pulled out some dollar bills from her purse and then gestured again toward the bill.

I pride myself on reading signs. I was certain that this American, before paying for my meal, wanted to be sure that I knew
exactly how much she was spending on me. Once this dawned on
me, I took the bill, held it away from my face, my brow furrowed
in feigned concentration. Convinced that I had met my benefactor's
bizarre expectation, I posted the bill back on the table. Then, turning again to Karen, I said, again, "Thank you."

She swiftly swept up the bill. She inclined it halfway in my
direction, as if there were not enough light and she had to slant the
paper so I could see it clearly. Then using her finger to underline
the point, she said to me, "You owe four dollars and twenty-five
cents—plus tip."

In an instant, my first meal with a "generous" American turned
into a moment of profound cultural disorientation. I was meant to
pay for a meal, even though she had suggested it—she had, in light
of my Nigerian cultural experience, freely offered me the meal?

My trouble was compounded. As a Nigerian, I didn't know
what "tip" meant. Nigerians do not tip. In fact, the whole idea
of paying more than the cost of my food struck me as absurd.
Far from paying more, Nigerians would quibble, haggle, and
harangue their way to a lower bill.

"Look here, madam," they might say, addressing a food seller.
"This your food no be am o. I no dey pay ten naira. Na only five I
dey pay."

"Customer, pay eight," the food vendor might say. "Next time,
I do you better."

"Six naira, no more, no less," the customer would offer.

"*Oya*, pay seven."

But the three-letter word "tip" was the least of my problems. I just found out I owed more than four dollars—and I didn't have a dime on me.

I felt too embarrassed to tell Karen that I had no money on me, and that I had presumed on her philanthropy. Caught in an awkward situation, I racked my brain for a way out that would save me some dignity. I stood up and began searching the pockets of my denim pants for what I knew wasn't there. I found nothing, as it was not a miracle day for me.

"I believe I left my money in Professor Nnaji's office," I lied to Karen. "Why don't you pay for both of us? Then we will return to Nnaji's office and I will give you my portion of the bill."

For the first time since I met her, an angry expression came over Karen's face. She seemed to wonder why on earth any person would go out to eat without having money in his pocket. Perhaps she regarded me as the world's most contemptible freeloader. Which was fine, for I thought even worse of her.

She paid, still seething, a closed look seizing her face. We walked back to Nnaji's office in unaccustomed, stunning silence. Karen didn't ask one question. I was preoccupied with how to find money to pay her, in no mood to chatter.

Nnaji's door was ajar, and I was relieved to find him in his office. In Igbo, I asked if I could have a word with him. He followed me just outside his office while Karen sat and waited.

"I'd like to borrow ten dollars," I said shortly, urgently, feeling it was best not to launch into any lengthy preamble.

A point of cultural information: Among Nigerians, asking a friend for "a loan"—especially of a small sum—was often a matter of polite form. Everybody, giver and taker alike, understood quite well that the money would likely never be repaid. Nnaji was not, by any strict definition, a friend of mine, but he was the Nigerian

I had grown closest to. Though I asked him for a loan, I might as well have said, *Give me the damn money.*

He obliged.

The cash in my hand swept away the embarrassment I had felt at the restaurant. With a sudden boost to my confidence, I called Karen out.

"In Nigeria," I said, in a didactic tone, "when you invite somebody out to eat, you imply an offer to pay for their meal."

"That's not how it's done in America," she replied, without missing a beat, as if she had anticipated me and had rehearsed that comeback.

"I just found out," I said, hoping that my face registered dismay, if not disgust. I held out the crisp ten-dollar bill Nnaji had given me. "Here's ten dollars. I'm paying for both of us today. But please, don't ever invite me again to eat, unless you're willing to pay."

She took the money and ran. I walked back into Nnaji's office.

"Do you know why I needed to borrow money?" I asked him. Then I told him of the drama at lunch.

Nnaji laughed and laughed. He stood up and sat back down and clapped and pounded the table and wiped tears with the back of his hand. At first curious, and then infected by his mirth, I laughed along.

At last, Nnaji collected himself. Regarding me with an amused expression, he said, "My brother, you've just been exposed to what Americans call going dutch."

"I'll continue to go Nigerian," I vowed, provoking him to another round of laughter.

(Since this experience, whenever an American friend invites me out to a restaurant, I always say, "Wait, there's a story." Then, after relating the "going dutch" narrative, I add, "The moral of the story is that I'm offering to pay, unless you insist." The story always elicits guffaws. In the interest of full disclosure, I might as well reveal that, most of the time, I get treated to a free breakfast, lunch, or dinner.)

DESPITE BEING UPSET WITH Karen over the lunch fiasco, I proceeded with my promise to help track down her father.

I rang C. Don up and told him the entire story about Karen's search for her father. He agreed to write a note for publication in one or two papers.

C. Don's note went awry. Instead of merely asking to be contacted by anybody who knew the whereabouts of Emmanuel U, he spilled the whole story. His note revealed that an American woman was looking for her father and then gave the man's name.

Within two days of the publication, Emmanuel U himself sent a terse note to C. Don. His tone was incensed. It must have seemed as if a ghost he thought he'd interred in the dim past intruded on his life. The rhythm of the life he had established for thirty years, apart from Karen's mother and Karen, had been rudely, unexpectedly upset. He demanded that C. Don obtain Karen's mother's name and Karen's date and place of birth. C. Don rang me with news of the latest development. Immediately, I contacted Karen. She seemed both ecstatic and anxious.

Satisfied that Karen was his daughter, Mr. U wrote directly to her. It was an unusual letter, compounded of acceptance and recrimination. It turned out that, on his return to Nigeria, the man had taken a job in the civil service. He had risen to the top of Nigeria's bureaucracy, and then retired. His natal community then chose him as their traditional ruler, a revered but largely ceremonial post.

In his letter to Karen, the man suggested that C. Don's letter in the newspaper was designed to embarrass him, to inflict grave emotional pain on him and his wife. Before he would establish any relationship with Karen, he insisted, his immediate trauma had to be addressed. In fact, he said members of his traditional cabinet demanded an explanation from everybody involved in the whole affair. That meant, above all, me.

My initial inclination was to declare myself done with the matter, in no mood to be drawn any further into a situation fast evolving into a tense, near-farcical drama. But Karen entreated me. She pleaded that I allay her father's suspicion that she, C. Don, and I had hatched a plan to tarnish his image—and cause him pain. If I didn't, she reminded me, the man would take it out on her, refuse to meet her. All her efforts, mine, as well as C. Don's, would be wasted.

I relented. I wrote a letter couched in a penitential tone to her father. I explained that there had not been any intent to debase him or wrinkle up his life. C. Don had simply made an innocent, if careless, mistake by adding details I had asked him not to share in the newspaper note.

My reassurance seemed to work magic. The man contacted Karen again, this time in a more conciliatory tone. In a few months, he said, he and his wife would be visiting Boston. Four of their children, all sons, lived in Boston or locations nearby. He would want to meet her during his visit.

Several months later, Karen rang to tell me her father was in Boston, and she was headed there to meet him and the rest of his family. She sounded excited, but I suspected she was also a bit apprehensive, just masking it. I was proud I had played a big role in solving her paternal puzzle, but I felt uneasy for her. For some odd—or altogether understandable—reason, my unease had to do with Karen's personality and appearance. She favored torn, bleached denim and sleeveless shirts that appeared purchased for next to nothing from some nth-power cast-off clothing store. She was sinewy skinny and loved to flex her arms and invite people to feel her steely muscles. I wondered how her cultivated bohemianism was going to play with her father, his wife, and their sons. Middle-class Nigerians tended to be more formal in their fashion choices. Many of them would frown on sartorial eccentricity.

Karen called me after her trip to Boston. Her voice, bereft of excitement, told all. Things had not gone quite as she'd imagined or hoped. One question had been answered: she had finally seen the resemblance between her biological father and herself. But the weightier question, whether there was a prospect of fashioning some vital, even usable, filial relationship—or how to go about it—hung in the air. The atmosphere in Boston was somber. Her father said she was welcome to visit him in Nigeria—if she could put the flight ticket together. Her father's wife stayed mostly distant, taciturn.

Karen's half brothers were not as reticent or guarded as their parents. The three oldest ones told Karen that the newspaper piece that called out their father had caused their mother undeserved pain. They had grown up with no inkling that Karen was somewhere out there, related to them by blood. It was too late, they told her, for them to get accustomed to the idea that she was their sister, indeed their oldest sibling. They had decided to move on with their lives apart from her, as if she had not, in a breathless bolt, bounded into their circle.

The youngest son made a different call. He hugged Karen and told her he treasured her as a sister.

FITTING THE DESCRIPTION

A round noon on Friday, December 23, 1988, I planted myself in front of a huddle of passengers underneath a Plexiglas-covered bus stop located close to the post office in the center of Amherst, Massachusetts. I was waiting for one of the Pioneer Valley Transit Authority buses that ran shuttles to destinations within Amherst and to surrounding towns. I was going to have a meeting with Bart Nnaji at his UMass office to discuss *African Commentary*.

I had been in America for a mere thirteen days. My body had made little progress habituating to the bone-piercing cold. Dressed for winter, I looked unaccustomedly bloated, ridiculously oversize in a fleece-lined winter jacket over several layers of shirts and a wool sweater. Gloved hands tucked inside the pockets of my jacket, I distracted myself by blowing air through my mouth. In those early days in America, I often entertained myself, when outside, by watching the stream of vapor that spooled from my mouth and nostrils.

I don't remember the trigger, but I suddenly raised my eyes at the traffic paused in front of the bus stop, waiting for the traffic light to turn. My eyes met the stare of a police officer waiting in his cruiser.

The instant our eyes met, I remembered my uncle's warning:

Americans did not stand for somebody looking them in the eye. And here I was, looking a police officer dead-on in the face. My heart quickened, jolted by fear. Immediately, I swept my eyes upward, as if some strange thing floating in the air had caught my attention. The gesture was swift and dramatic. It was a word-less way of assuring the officer that, in locking eyes with him, ever briefly, I had not meant any provocation. I needed him to realize that I had made an innocent mistake, committed an inadvertent act.

Even though I had quickly averted my gaze, I still monitored the officer's vehicle with the corner of my eye. The traffic light turned green. The officer pulled forward and then turned right onto a street beside the post office. I heaved a sigh of relief worthy of a man who had dodged a bullet.

A minute or so later, I felt the pressure of a hand on my shoulder. I whirled around—to the sight of a police uniform! Images of my bullet-riddled body flashed through my mind. My heart-beat cranked up. My legs felt leaden. Something was choking my throat, drying my mouth.

"Sir, do you mind stepping out to the back of the bus stop?" I heard the officer say.

His words threw me into cultural disorientation. I had just arrived, less than two weeks earlier, from Nigeria, a country where no man in any kind of uniform, much less a police officer, would address an "idle" civilian as "sir." No, not even as a joke. When a Nigerian police officer called you sir, it meant that he was being truly deferential to you. Indeed, to so address you meant he was fully, unctuously, at your service. And no Nigerian police officer would use the phrase "do you mind?" In Nigeria, the police were more wont to push, pull, or shove you where they wanted you.

For a moment, then, the officer's odd phrase gave me an injec-tion of confidence, restored a smidgen of calm to my nerves. The combination of "sir" and "do you mind?" translated, I imagined, into a relationship where the officer was somehow subservient, and

I superior. His language gave me the illusion of having a choice in the matter. I thought I could say to him, *Actually, I'm rather in a hurry to a meeting. I'd be happy to make your acquaintance some other day. Certainly, not today.*

Yet, a part of me was both curious and impressed by the officer's genteel air, his beguiling words. I was open to the encounter, willing to meet him immediately.

"I don't mind," I said, picking my way from the crowded bus stop.

Once behind the Plexiglas-framed bus stop, the officer and I faced each other. A tall and sturdy man, the officer folded his arms, looking down on me as if from Mount Olympus. I fixed my eyes on his broad chest.

"Sir, you know what this is about, right?" he asked.

I knew. Of course, I knew. I knew exactly what I had done to wrong this officer—a mini-giant of a man whose gun, holstered to his hip, both added to his towering advantage and reminded me of the trigger-happy dudes in westerns. I had not the slightest confusion about the precise nature of my sin against the officer. I had committed that most un-American of acts: I had looked him in the eye! And I knew better. My uncle had duly warned me. And I had spent the previous thirteen days scrupulously avoiding looking Americans in the eye. But my eyes, unaccountably, had wandered, betrayed me. It was all a sinister plot by the ocular part of me against the whole of me.

And then, here I was.

I knew. But the last thing I was going to do was confess. For a confession would amount to empowering the officer to shoot me. Denial was my only option. After all, I didn't know the man's temperament. I could not trust that he would be assuaged if I admitted to my wrongdoing but then apologized, explained that I had not acted willfully. I would not take any risks. In the event, my safest bet was resolute, interminable denial.

"No, I don't know what this is about." The words seemed to scratch their way out of my dry, choked throat.

"Sir, are you sure you don't know?" the officer asked again.

A moment of doubt crept in. Was the officer offering me a last opportunity to confess and receive absolution and warning? Did I dare confess?

"I really don't know," I said, determined to stick to my policy.

"There's been a bank robbery," the officer said. "You fit the description."

It was as if the earth beneath me had suddenly shifted, left me doddering. I was aware that everybody at the bus stop had turned, gazing at me, eavesdropping. I had the sensation of being spun round and round by some demonic force. My head pounded; my heart beat harder, ever faster. Tears welled up in my eyes, but I dared not wipe them. I *had* to speak, I needed to speak, but I was like a man struck with muteness. For a moment, I was tempted to raise my eyes to the officer, hoping he possessed the art of reading innocence on my face. I squelched the idea; better not to compound my troubles by adding the provocation of looking the officer in the eye.

A part of me wanted to laugh, a plain, artless laugh that would be commensurate with the absurdity of the situation. Of all possible responses, laughter, odd as it might at first appear, seemed most fitting, if not logical. If I had wanted to rob a bank in America, I certainly would have needed a lot more prep time. Would I not have reconnoitered my target to figure out the bank's layout? Would I not have seen to acquiring such instruments as a gun and a ski mask? Would I not have taken time to recruit an accomplice or two and to arrange a decent getaway? What kind of idiot would rob a bank and then go plant himself—as if in self-exhibition—in a huddle at a bus stop? It all seemed terribly, hilariously ludicrous.

My speech, as if by magic, returned. And I began to speak with diarrheic velocity. I told the officer I had been in America only thirteen days, I had not been inside any American bank, I was in town to edit an international magazine, I had never stolen anything of value from anybody, much less robbed a bank, I was on my way to see a professor at UMass to talk about the magazine I was in town to edit.

"Sir," the officer said, interrupting my verbal torrent. "Do you have identification?"

"No."

"No? Why not?"

I explained again that I had just arrived from Nigeria approximately two weeks before. My only ID was my international passport. I didn't think it was safe to carry it on me wherever I went; I could lose it.

"Sir, do you mind if I frisk you?"

Frisk? The word was not part of my vocabulary at the time. Even though the officer had once again employed that phrase "do you mind?" I detected that a certain gruff quality had crept into his voice. Somehow I knew that, whatever "frisk" meant, I had little or no choice in the matter.

"No," I offered.

"Put your hands above your heads, sir."

I complied. The officer began to pat me down. He began from my shoulder blades, then worked his way carefully down to my stomach, my back, my hip, then farther down to the calves and ankles. As he pressed and kneaded my jacket, I could sense the slightest agitation in him, a certain tenseness in his features, as if he was poised for any surprise move I might make. I tried to stand still, rigid as a wooden statue, but all of me shook hideously, everything in me repulsed by the groping I had apparently consented to, yet helpless.

Convinced I had no weapons, the officer relaxed.

"Do you mind if I drive you to your residence?" he asked. "I'd like to see your passport."

Pure terror seized me. Back in Nigeria, I had heard stories about police driving suspects in serious crimes to some isolated spot and shooting them dead. "Wasting" was the name for this illicit morbid act. I always considered the practice barbaric, inexcusable, but some Nigerians did not share my abhorrence. Years ago, before relocating to the United States, I had debated the issue with a man who announced his enthusiastic endorsement of the policy. According to this interlocutor, extrajudicial execution was a calculated preemptive strike against the machinations of clever defense lawyers. Some lawyers loved money so much they'd consent to defend just about anybody, including certified murderers. And these lawyers, he said, had too many legal tricks up their sleeves for the good of society. In court, the lawyers could deploy one mesmeric legal maneuver or another to spring their clients free, even when the odds were that these clients were capital felons.

To obviate criminals' access to certain lawyers' legal wizardry, the Nigerian police—the open secret was widely whispered—would sometimes decide it was their duty to arrest, prosecute, and execute. Despite occasional reports on the incessancy of this horrific act, few people voiced revulsion. Perhaps many Nigerians bought the argument that the larger good of society was served. And this ostensible social profit justified the recourse to a crude, extraordinary, state-sponsored—or, at the very least, state-ignored—murder. In some quarters, it was viewed less as an egregious violation of the principle that presumed the accused innocent until their guilt was properly established than as an oddly wholesome insurance against the potent shenanigans of lawyers versed in the art of securing acquittals.

What if the Amherst police officer drove me to an isolated spot in town and, with nobody to witness the dastardly act, simply "wasted" me? The fear assumed solid, disquieting shape. In silence, I contemplated my next move. A part of me wanted to sprint away. I had been a notable track athlete in high school. I was confident of outrunning the police officer. But the sight of the officer's gun froze me. Even if the man couldn't catch up, how was I to outstrip his bullet? Another option: shriek, wail, create a scene, do whatever it took to invite all those people at the bus stop eyeing the officer and me to rush to my aid. But what if I started my racket and everybody remained indifferent? What if they chose to watch from a safe distance as the officer had his way with me? At any rate, my sense of dignity kicked in. If I was going to be shot, better to go down with my dignity intact.

In the end, there was only one option: compliance. Even if the officer harbored horrific designs, perhaps he would take due note of my willingness to do as he commanded.

"I don't mind," I said.

The officer motioned me into the backseat of his cruiser. As he drove toward my residence, he radioed the office to announce he'd picked up a suspect who had no identification. He was driving to my residential address to take a look at my passport.

I was greatly relieved when he pulled up outside 38 Prospect Street. After unlocking the car to let me out, he stayed a step or two behind as we walked to the front door.

Chinua Achebe's two younger children, Chidi and Nwando, both students at UMass, were in the house for their Christmas break. They were alarmed to see a police officer walk in with me.

"I have been arrested for bank robbery," I explained to them in Igbo language.

They were duly astonished, speechless.

"My passport is upstairs," I told the officer.

"Go get it," he ordered.

I went up, fetched the passport, and handed it to the officer. He examined it for a while and then began to make entries on a small machine. Several minutes later, he gave me back the passport.

"Thanks for being a gentleman," he said.

As he turned to leave, I remembered that many people had seen him question me, search me, zoom away with me in the back of the cruiser. For sure, any of these spectators, whenever they saw me in town, could point me out to their friends and say, "This guy here is some kind of criminal. I don't know what he did exactly, but I saw a cop pick him up."

The prospect of that notoriety dimmed my elation at being cleared.

"Do you mind dropping me back off at the bus stop?" I asked the officer.

It was a tactical move. I figured that other people would be there at the bus stop to see me step out of the cruiser and wave my thanks as the officer drove away. At the very least, when somebody pointed to me and said, "There's a criminal there. I saw him get arrested at a bus stop," chances would be that another witness would testify, "But I saw an officer drop him off at the same spot."

"No problem at all," the officer said.

As I hastened off, I forgot to tell Chidi and Nwando that I had been cleared, the officer having determined that I wasn't the suspect.

I arrived at Professor Nnaji's office more than an hour after our scheduled appointment. The door was open—in fact, he often left it that way—but he wasn't in. I sat down to wait, convinced he had gone to teach a class or attend some meeting.

An hour or so later, the professor breezed in. He stopped sharply, astounded to see me.

"When did you get here?" he asked. He angled his face to look at me, as if he couldn't quite believe I was right there in front of him. His expression was harried. It was the dead of winter, but a film of sweat covered his face.

"About an hour ago," I said.

Chidi Achebe had telephoned to alert him that I had been arrested for bank robbery. He jumped in his car and raced to Amherst police station. The officer he met there insisted there was nobody in custody with my name. Nnaji zipped to a police station in a neighboring town. Again, the police gave the same response: they had detained nobody bearing my name. He checked with the police at yet another town; it was the same story. Confused, he drove back to Amherst. There, a police officer said politely, but firmly, that I had not turned up.

Nnaji went to a pay phone and called Chidi and Nwando. They swore they had seen me being driven away in a vehicle marked AMHERST POLICE. Convinced that the police were playing some diabolical game, Nnaji warned them that he had two solid witnesses, and he was going to contact an attorney. Indeed, he had breezed into his office to check his Rolodex for a certain lawyer's telephone number.

And there I was, waiting!

I don't believe the Amherst police ever arrested the actual bank robber. On December 24, 1988, a day after the robbery, the *Hampshire Gazette*, based in Northampton, Massachusetts, carried a report under a sedate headline: BANK IN AMHERST ROBBED. The report stated, *Police Friday night were searching for a bandit who pulled off a daring holdup at the Heritage-NIS Bank in the center of town Friday.*

The robber entered the South Pleasant Street bank at 10:42 a.m. and pushed a teller a note that said he had a gun and wanted money. The paper reported that the police declined to disclose how much money the robber received, but *William Stapleton, senior vice president at Heritage-NIS, would only say that the amount stolen "was a minor amount."* The report continued: *Carrying the money in a large manila envelope, the suspect fled the area on foot . . .*

Although there have been numerous "sightings" from all over Amherst, none have led to an arrest. The paper added that several witnesses had told police that the suspect was *a light-skinned black man, approximately 28 years old, of medium build. Amherst police said the man probably wore glasses and may have had a mustache and freckles.*

Witnesses further described the suspect as having either a black and blue mark, a scar or a birthmark under his left eye. The man was reportedly wearing a tan cap, tan coat, white shirt, and brown pants.

On December 27, 1988, the *Gazette* reported again on the unsolved crime. Headlined BANK VIDEO CAMERA FILMED HOLDUP SUSPECT, the report remarked that a *composite sketch of the man—put together through interviews with eyewitnesses—shows a well-dressed, light-skinned black man, 25 to 30 years old, wearing a light tan wool cap, brown pants, and a thigh-length tan jacket.*

The next day, December 28, the *Amherst Bulletin*, a weekly newspaper, gave the suspect, if not the robbery, a livelier headline: WELL-DRESSED MAN ROBS AMHERST BANK. The paper reported: *A well-dressed robber who took an undisclosed sum of money from a bank across the common from the Amherst police station on Friday was still being sought Tuesday morning, according to police. Police said the man gave a bank teller a note saying he had a gun and then left the Heritage-NIS Bank on South Pleasant Street with cash in a yellow envelope.* The *Bulletin* reported that bank personnel *described the suspect as a freck-led, 5-foot 7-inch black man, about 25 years of age.*

Years later, revisiting the whole experience by tracking down reports of the robbery in local newspapers, I was intrigued, above all, that the suspect and I shared some brackets—in age, skin tone, and the higher estimates of his height.

Besides, I had told the story of my interrogation for the robbery so many times in the intervening years that I could not help noting how my mood, my perspective of the event, had shifted over time. In the early years, I had let the sense of dread I felt overwhelm my narrative. But as time passed, I learned to relax. I refined a more relaxed accent for the story, a mode that juxtaposed my memory of terror with the sheer absurdity of it—hence the humor, the hilarity.

The same kind of spirit informed my response to the newspaper accounts. I focused on the slight variations, inflections, and modu-lations between one paper and the other. The *Gazette*'s headline left the impression of yawning at the robber's exploits. By contrast, the

Bulletin's rendered the man somewhat endearing, made him personable, a man of sartorial taste who—perhaps on a whim—made a dash to rob a bank located within whistling distance of a police station, as if that act were organic to the concerns of "well-dressed" men everywhere or were (at worst) a brief digression from his otherwise lofty, gentlemanly repertoire. Unlike the *Gazette*, which reported the suspect at five feet ten inches, the weekly paper scaled the man back some—leaving him at five feet seven inches.

In a way, this mysterious, freckled bank robber has stayed with me all these years later. It was like having an evil twin brother you never met, but who went around doing sinister deeds, getting you into vicarious trouble. There were times when I felt bitter toward him, when I resented the fact that his appalling choice had caused me great grief. Not anymore. Over time, a certain curiosity overcame the resentment, erased the bitterness.

No, I will never be nostalgic about that moment when I stood cowering before that tall Amherst police officer. But that encounter also gave me a great story—a strange, unintended gift from that well-dressed, freckled loser. And here I am, all those years later, still standing, even stronger, in many ways still a pilgrim just arrived from Nigeria, except that I am also in many definite ways more of an American than I was back then.

And I am not about to exchange that gift for anything.

ARE YOU OKAY?

One of the great delights of my early days in the United States was that Amherst, my first address in the country, teemed with Africans.

The Africans' presence buoyed me. I had uprooted myself from Nigeria, the one place I'd known all my life, and planted myself in a different soil. It is hard to convey the joy, the comfort and magic of seeing, everywhere I turned, people who had the same tone of skin, who spoke English with an accent, ate the kind of food I loved, whose lives were, perhaps, animated by similar dreams.

I hadn't quite figured out how to relate to Americans, that strange tribe that went around with guns and—I believed—would shoot you for looking them in the eye.

The Africans were from different places. Most were Nigerians, but there were also Togolese, Ghanaians, Liberians, South Africans, Senegalese, and so on. Whatever their nationality, they were—like me—arrivistes of one sort or another. To some degree—or so I presumed—they and I shared a few social experiences as well as cultural traits and habits. In their company, I could let my guard down, find a measure of tranquility, share rich, spicy food, tell jokes, and crackle with loud, careless laughter. I developed an instinct for detecting Africans merely by sight. Sometimes I got it wrong, but I was oftener right.

One day, I stood outside the entrance to Amherst Books looking at a display of clearance books. Glancing up, I noticed that a bronze-skinned man with a groomed look stood next to me. He, too, was examining the racks filled with used books. I conjectured that he was African.

I was about to speak to him when he met my gaze, nodded, and smiled broadly. I offered a warm smile of my own.

He extended his hand. "Ike Peloewetse," he said.

"Okey," I said, taking his hand. "Okey Ndibe."

He began to laugh.

"It's really my name," I assured him, believing he found my name hard to believe.

My assurance only made him roar with greater laughter. He continued to laugh as I stood, watching him, mildly amused by his reaction.

Among the Igbo of Nigeria, Okey—which is short for Okechukwu—is a fairly common name. It is pronounced like the word "okay," but with a slightly longer stretch of the second syllable. During my years in Nigeria, there was never one instant when my name was considered odd or funny. By contrast, in America my name provoked incredulity and hilarity. I, too, adopted the spirit, often using my name to play pranks on people.

Ike laughed for several minutes, bent over. At first, I was puzzled. Then I began to laugh too, a reaction that seemed to fuel him even more.

"Man, you won't believe what happened yesterday," he said, after he composed himself and wiped tear-filled eyes with the back of his hand.

"I can't wait to hear it," I said eagerly, even though it was clear he didn't need spurring.

He had gone grocery shopping at the Stop & Shop located on

Route 9. As he pushed his cart down an aisle, a white woman approached from the opposite direction. As they passed each other, their eyes met. It was a brief encounter. Yet, he recalled a certain intense interest in her eyes, encouraging the impression that, somehow, something meaningful had passed between them. He smiled at her. She returned a smile rendered radiant by her searching eyes. Rather than go on her merry shopping way, she paused, compelling him to reciprocate.

"How do you like the snow?" she asked, sweeping her arm in the direction of the parking lot.

A succession of snowstorms had blanketed the streets with whiteness, deposited banks of snow everywhere, conscripting much of the grocery store's parking lot.

"I hate snowstorms," he protested. "I like it warm and dry."

"You have an accent. Where're you from?"

"Botswana."

"Is that in Africa?" she asked.

"Yes."

"Are you okay?"

"Yes."

The woman seemed inclined to tarry even longer. As other shoppers maneuvered around them, Ike said, he and the woman stood there, like long friends, talking. The woman asked about his impressions of America. And she asked a few questions about Africa. As he spoke, he discerned in her demeanor something akin to absorption. He felt flattered by her attentiveness.

They had talked for at least fifteen minutes when the woman said, "Wow, I can't believe you're okay."

He was taken aback. "Is there anything about me that suggests I'm not okay?" he asked.

"No," the woman assured. "But it's just that I've heard several stories about you."

"You have?" he asked, bewildered.

"Yes," the woman said with a confident smile.

"Like what story?"

"I know you're in town to set up an international magazine."

The whole thing seemed to him farcical. "That's not true," he said, a little too hotly. "I'm here as a graduate student."

"But you said you were okay," the woman said in a tone that approached remonstration.

"Yes, I'm fine."

The woman covered her face with two hands in a gesture of shame. Then, shaking her head from side to side, she said, "Oh my gosh, I'm so, so sorry. There's a guy in town whose name is Okey. He's in Amherst to edit a magazine. When I asked if you were Okey, I meant his name—not 'okay.' I'm so sorry, but I thought I was speaking to this guy, Okey."

It was an awkward turn, and for him ridiculous and extremely irritating. As he and the apologetic woman went their separate ways, he seethed with fury. He replayed the entire encounter in his mind. Its import was clear to him. No question, the woman had initially intended to pick him up. He was willing to be picked up. But—so he surmised—the woman had changed her mind midway through the rite of seduction. And she had come up with some yarn, an infantile one at that, about an editor named Okey, pronounced "okay."

Ike had thought: What a pathetic liar!

Then the day after that weird encounter with his would-be seducer, Ike and I met outside a bookstore. Once I introduced myself, everything came together for him. He realized that I was a flesh-and-blood proper noun named Okey. The woman at Stop & Shop had not, after all, invented some ruse to enable her to find an escape route from the object of a desire gone suddenly cold.

We became instant pals, our friendship forged by the story of a day when my name created a double illusion. He was a single father of two daughters and a son. He was an excellent cook and often invited me to join his family at meals. Often, in the middle of a chat or a meal, he would roll out in laughter. Afterward, he would retell the whole uproarious story.

One day, Ike and I were strolling just outside the main library at UMass when he saw an African American woman, a fellow graduate student who was in the same course.

Ike introduced the woman to me. Then he said to her, "He's Okey."

She flipped her head back and then gave him a sharp, scolding look. "Why you telling me that?" she asked.

"He's Okey," Ike repeated, feigning obliviousness to her bellicose attitude.

One hand on her hip, the woman swayed her head from side to side. "You hardly know me. And I'm not even looking. Where do you come off telling me a guy I never met before is okay?" she asked.

I was on the verge of guffawing but reined it in. Ike was a master of the art of facial plasticity.

"He's really Okey," he said in a strong, insistent tone, motioning in my direction.

The woman had heard enough. She rebuked Ike for his bad manners, announced she felt disrespected that he would declare a guy she was just meeting okay for her. And she spiced the message with a liberal dose of curses.

Seeing her worked up, Ike smiled. "I wasn't playing romantic matchmaker," he said. "I introduced you to the guy. I thought you'd like to know him as well. His name is Okey. It's spelled O-k-e-y."

The woman looked at me with a doubtful expression. I nodded.

"No," she said, eyes darting from Ike to me, as if trying to figure out whether we were tag-team pranksters. "He's bullshitting, right?"

"Actually that's my name."

"I don't believe it for a minute."

I gave an affirming smile. "Trust me; it's true."

"I need to see your driver's license."

I produced my license. As she inspected it, disbelief eased away from her face. She covered her face, exclaiming, "Oh my God! Oh my God!" Ike broke out into laughter. I joined in. And then the woman followed suit.

Soon, still overcome with laughter, she clasped me in an embrace. "I'm so sorry," she said. "You got you a unique name. And here I was thinking the brother was telling me you were *okay* for me!"

★   ★   ★

A NORWEGIAN "OKAY" INTERLUDE

In late September 2009, I traveled to Trondheim, Norway, to attend the Nordic Africa Days conference. The Nordic Africa Institute, based in Uppsala, Sweden, was my sponsor. In December 2006, the institute had invited me to Uppsala, where I joined several African and European writers at a symposium tagged "Creative Writers' Workshop on War and Peace in Africa." Soon after the symposium, the institute commissioned the Zimbabwean writer Chenjerai Hove and me to edit the presentations for publication. The resultant book, *Writers Writing on Conflicts and Wars in Africa*, was published in 2009. It was to be officially launched at the Nordic Africa Days conference, which was why the institute was flying me to Norway. My flight itinerary, on Icelandair, went from New York City to Reykjavík, the capital of Iceland, to the Norwegian capital, Oslo, and then on a one-hour shuttle to Trondheim.

A week before my trip, I received an email from Nina Klinge-Nygård of the Nordic Africa Institute. Her own flight would arrive in Trondheim thirty minutes ahead of mine, Nina wrote. Then she added: *I will be there waiting for you . . . I figure we might as well go together on the bus to the hotel.*

But just in case her schedule or mine went awry, she sent me another email with the following instruction: *The airport is a*

30–40-minute drive from the town center and the conference hotels. The easiest way to reach your hotel is by the airport express bus, which corresponds with every arrival at Trondheim Airport Værnes. The bus stand is to your right when you exit the terminal building. A one-way ticket costs NOK 90, and you may pay by credit card on the bus. When you reach the town center, the stops will be announced.

The shuttle aircraft from Oslo arrived in Trondheim, as scheduled, at 4:35 P.M. on September 30, 2009. During the flight into Trondheim, it dawned on me that Nina and I had never met each other. I couldn't tell her apart in a room of several white women. For that matter, but for the fact that I was black, she too would have a hard time identifying me. She had not attended the workshops during my 2006 visit to Uppsala. I feared that she and I might miss each other.

The fear went away as the plane approached the runway. Looking out the window, I saw the airport building, relatively small. The odds were slim that we would miss each other in such a space.

The baggage-claim belt was next to a small lounge where a smattering of people, men and women, sat, perhaps waiting for arriving passengers. My suitcase rolled out quickly. I grabbed it and then made a round of the lounge, making sure that every woman in the lounge made eye contact with me. None of them sprang up to welcome me. I concluded that Nina's flight from Sweden must be late.

I exited the airport, looked to my right, and saw an idling bus. I paid ninety Norwegian kroner and settled in a seat just behind the driver, but on the other side of the aisle. I got down when the driver announced the stop for Rica Nidelven Hotel. At the hotel's front desk, I gave my name and was courteously checked in.

Later that evening, I met Nina at the ballroom where the book I coedited was officially launched. The hall was parked with conference participants. Our interaction was brief, but her charisma and jocularity were on display. She apologized for missing me at the airport, but offered no explanation. There was little time.

It rained incessantly during the three days I spent in Trondheim. Despite the wetness, the book presentation was glitch-free. Chenjerai and I reignited an intense, bantering friendship that started on our first meeting in Uppsala. I went out drinking, eating, and sightseeing with several African and European scholars. I attended a few conference sessions and heard a marvelous keynote speech by the eminent Swedish novelist Henning Mankell. I met Disa Hastad, a heavyset Swedish journalist of magisterial bearing whose passion for Africa was as strong as her writing on the continent was penetrating. I was flattered to learn that she followed my newspaper columns. We spent some time discussing Nigeria's prospects and its confounding ways.

The second day of the conference, Hastad coaxed me into forgoing a panel I had planned to attend. "Do you know about the Nidaros Cathedral?" she asked. "It's quite impressive, a major monument here. I'm going to see it. Come with me."

We took a bus that stopped a short distance from the majestic cathedral. The moment we alighted, a heavy downpour descended on us. Disa walked with a cane, her bad leg forcing her to keep to a plodding pace. I expected her to suggest that we duck under the bus-stop shelter or some building until the rain ceased. Instead, as she walked with a pronounced limp, she turned to look at me. She laughed, apparently amused by my bunched body, bowed head, and grimace. In a stentorian air that carried over the clatter, she declaimed, "Rain is not going to kill us." I was too drenched, too helpless, to argue the point.

I had a marvelous time in Trondheim, savored the rich harvest of contacts made, insights gained, sights beheld. On October 3, 2009, I boarded a flight and left rainy Norway.

ON JANUARY 11, 2010, I received an intriguing email from Nina. She wrote: *I do have a report to give you on what happened in Trondheim,*

something I was too ashamed to tell when there. Email doesn't do justice to
my story, better to do it over the phone. Please let me know when I can call
you (it'll have to be afternoon here) and to which number.

Several days later, I emailed her my mobile number. On January
18, 2010, she wrote: Nemas problemas! *I'll call you tomorrow, Tues-*
day . . . Don't expect too much.

Here's the story she told.

She had indeed been waiting at the airport in Trondheim when
my flight arrived. Once my flight's arrival was announced, she ran
to the bathroom to spruce up. By the time she reemerged to look
for me, I had already made the rounds of the lounge—and then left
on the bus, headed for the hotel.

She didn't imagine I could have picked up my luggage and left
so quickly; she conjectured I had missed my connecting flight from
Oslo. Since another connecting flight was due in about an hour, she
elected to wait for it.

There was a lone black man on the next flight that arrived from
Oslo. She approached him, smiled, and asked, "Are you Okey?"

"Yes," the man replied.

"Did you miss your connecting flight from Oslo?"

"I did, yes."

"So sorry," she told him. "Get your luggage, let's go."

He grabbed his luggage and walked out with her to the bus. She
paid the fare for both of them, and they sat next to each other. During the bus ride to the city, she kept trying to draw the man out
into conversing. He was taciturn and seemed somewhat uncomfortable, even a tad pained, by her attention. This confused her a
bit; her colleagues who had met me in Uppsala in 2006 had por-
trayed me as a gregarious person with a penchant for telling stories.
She put the man's sour mien down to a long, torturous flight and
the fact he had missed one connecting flight.

The bus stopped at a location near the hotel, and she bid the man
follow her. At the front desk, she introduced herself in Norwegian

and was duly checked in. Then, motioning in the direction of the man who stood behind her, she asked the hotel clerk to check in "Okey Ndibe."

The clerk peered into the computer and announced, "Okey Ndibe already checked in."

"Not possible," she said testily. "He's right here with me."

The clerk was adamant that I had checked in.

Nina demanded to talk to the manager. She complained that his front-desk clerk was refusing to check me in. The manager dithered, peered at a computer screen, brows furrowed as he clicked. Then he gave her a suspicious look. "Madam, our records show that Okey Ndibe is already our guest," he said in the tone of a man burdened with driving home a point to an irrationally incredulous person.

Vexed both by that tone and what she took as some irritating computer glitch, she turned to the man behind her and ordered, "Please tell them your name is Okey Ndibe."

The man shrugged. "That's not my name."

"What?" she uttered. "I asked you at the airport whether you were Okey and you said yes,"

"You asked if I was okay, and I said yes, I was," the man responded, in turn regarding her with an expression of suspicion.

Suddenly, the absurdity of her error hit her. She couldn't decide whether to laugh or to cry. She began to explain the mix-up both to the hotel staff, in Norwegian, and the man she had ensnared from the airport, in English. Everybody felt a measure of awkwardness but also great relief.

The man she had mistaken for me turned out to be a Ghanaian scholar, in Trondheim for the same "Nordic Africa Days" conference. Of course, he had not expected to be picked up at the airport. When Nina had asked him at the airport to follow her, he had been surprised but pleased. He'd taken it as an act of Norwegian hospitality.

Nina said she'd not told me the story in Trondheim for fear that I would be upset. Back in Uppsala, her colleagues at the Nordic Africa Institute pressed her to share the story with me. She demurred, even though her colleagues assured her I would be thrilled. It took a while before she came round and then decided to send me that email asking for my phone number.

I told Nina how grateful I was for the gift of another "Okay" story, a Scandinavian angle on a familiar experience with my name.

ON A CROC'S BACK, AMERICA-BOUND

often went to visit Professor Bart Nnaji either at his office at the University of Massachusetts Amherst or at his robotics lab, just outside the engineering department building. On one visit, I met Chris, a graduate student of engineering who seemed endlessly curious about Nigeria and Africa. On seeing me, Chris would exclaim "Okey!" and invariably take a break from his work to chat. He had a sense of humor and would often commence laughing at his own joke even before he had finished making it. He also had a way of standing with one hand on his hip, his body tipped slightly forward, head cocked toward me, leaving the impression of intense interest in my responses to his barrage of questions.

One afternoon, having found Nnaji's office locked, I walked down the stairs and out the engineering building to see if he was in his lab. As I walked in, Chris looked up from poring over an engineering textbook. As was his wont, he shouted my name and smiled widely.

"Professor Nnaji here?" I asked, even though I had a clear view of the lab and could see that Chris was alone.

"He was here earlier. Did you check his office?"

"He wasn't there."

"He's probably in class. Or in a meeting. Did you check with the secretary?"

I explained I didn't; it wasn't that important.

"Glad you came," Chris said. "I've got a question for you."

"Go ahead," I urged.

"I've been wondering about something. I see a lot of Africans around town. How are you guys able to come to America when there are no airports in Africa?"

Chris was fond of rib-cracking jokes, a tendency to roll out a hard, easy laugh. I searched his face. There was not a trace of amusement, no sign of laughter reined in. Yet, I conjectured, he must have spoken in jest. Perhaps I was seeing a new side of him, a rookie funnyman, trying out his material on me. I let out a quick laugh but stopped when he didn't join me. Briefly, I scrutinized his face again. I reckoned it closed, inscrutable. That he was serious seemed to me an implausible scenario. Despite the absence of clues on his face, I regarded his question as a joke. At any rate, I was going to respond as if his question had been asked in a comedic spirit.

I said, "Why, we ride on the backs of crocodiles across the Atlantic!"

Instantly, an expression of horror seized his face. "Crocodiles? Don't they eat you?"

This time, his genius for disguise impressed me. I was determined to sustain the lighthearted tone. "Oh no," I assured. "African languages make crocodiles docile. If you speak an African language, a crocodile would give you a hug. Even kiss you, if you wanted."

"Wow!" Chris exclaimed. His mouth hung open. This time, his eyes appeared to search mine. "Amazing!"

Later that night, I received a telephone call from Chris. "Okey, I told the crocodile story to my roommates, but they don't believe it. I'd like you to meet them. They need to hear the story from the horse's mouth." He sounded unquestioningly serious. Yet, I was not about to abandon my tone of levity.

"I don't know the horse that well," I said. "And the crocodile I know rather better is too busy ferrying other Africans across the Atlantic."

I was quite shocked to realize that Chris had not been joking all along, as I had thought. It was then that the hilarious potential of the conversation struck me. I couldn't help imagining a most absurdist scene at New York Harbor, wave after wave of African immigrants arriving after a wearying trip on the backs of crocodiles, their luggage wrapped in water-soaked bundles. I pictured US immigration agents processing these new immigrants who'd braved the perils of tumultuous seas.

When I told a few African friends about my exchanges with Chris, one of them remarked, "It makes sense that crocodiles bring us to America. As far as some Americans are concerned, animals are *the* first natives of Africa."

Several years later, my father-in-law, Aliyu Babatunde Fafunwa, told me kindred stories from the 1950s when he was a student at Bethune-Cookman College in Florida. His stories were every bit as fantastical as mine. And he told them with the same self-deprecatory sense of humor that served me and many other Africans.

One day, an American student had asked him, "Is it true that you Africans live in trees?"

"Yes, that's where we live," he'd answered, nodding vigorously.

"So how do you get up there?"

"We take the elevator, of course!"

On another occasion, somebody had asked him, "What do you Africans do when an elephant storms into your home in the jungle?"

"You have very little choice when an elephant decides to call. First, you pull out the best chair you have. Then you look up at the mammoth thing. Then, gesturing in the direction of the chair, you say, 'Mr. Elephant, please make yourself at home.'"

On yet another occasion, shortly after his arrival in Florida, a

professor at Bethune-Cookman had invited the small contingent
of African students to his house for dinner. Ravenously hungry, my
father-in-law and his fellow guests had looked forward to gorging on
a sumptuous, home-cooked meal. In the American tradition, dinner was preceded by a long, meandering conversation over cheese
and crackers. The preamble served to sharpen their appetites. Finally,
dinner was served, and they were summoned to the table.

Right before their eyes was a meal of salad, steak, boiled potatoes, and sautéed vegetables. Much of it looked unpromisingly
bland. But that was the least of the problem. The steak on the
platter was rare. Blood seemed to surge out of it, coloring meat
and plate alike. They had never seen cooked meat awash with
blood. They sat staring at the strange sight, too horrified to touch
the food. It was an extremely awkward moment, made worse
because they had little or no idea how to draw their host's attention, with delicate politeness, to the fact that he had presented
them with meat that wasn't cooked.

At length, their professor noticed that they were not eating.
"Go ahead, boys, eat your dinner," he prodded.

It was my father-in-law who finally found his voice. Speaking
gingerly, haltingly, he said, "Sir, I think the meat has not been
cooked. There is, um, a lot of blood in it."

"What!" the teacher cried. "I expected that you Africans would
worry that the meat was cooked at all."

A week or two after I sold the crocodile yarn to Chris, Kitty
Axelson, then the editor of the *Valley Advocate,* a free newspaper that provided the kind of political and art features and news
ignored by America's mainstream media, asked me to write an
opinion piece of my choice for her paper. I focused on some Americans' bizarre impressions of Africa as the charmed kingdom of
animals, the human population sometimes deemed marginal, even
an inconvenient intrusion on an idyllic, wild landscape. I recounted
my conversation with Chris.

When the piece was published, I gave Chris a copy. I watched, bemused, as he read it. Raising his face from the paper, he gave me an embarrassed smile. Then, as the smile widened, he grabbed me by the collar of my shirt.

"Gosh, so you lied to me! You lied to me!" he screamed, good-naturedly.

What was it about Africa that enabled some Americans to, in effect, regard the continent as some form of pathology, on the one hand simple and stark and digestibly knowable, on the other mysterious, spellbindingly magical, remote? How many times did Americans tell me they had an African friend I must know, their confidence based on the fact that their friend's father was an important man in Africa, a lawyer, say, or a dentist? And then, as if they believed that Africa was some small village, rather than a continent of fifty-plus countries, they would mention a name that rang a bell only because I had read numerous novels by different African writers and could conjecture that the name given to me was, in all likelihood, from some East African country, say. How many times was I asked how it was sleeping in Africa at night, with all that racket from lions, baboons, and monkeys, to say nothing of the slithering venomous snakes and a myriad nameless gnomes and goblins?

Why was it easy to render Africa as some utterly "other" location, a space devoid of logic and order, indeed a habitat where simplicities, mayhems, chimeras, and other incredible phenomena take root, sprout to life, thrive?

In the twin decades of the 1980s and 1990s, America saw the germination among black Americans of an intense renewal of interest in Africa. It expressed itself, this Afrocentric consciousness, in a certain buoyant identification with Africa, especially its ancient civilizations and kingdoms, pharaonic Egypt chief among them. But that awakening was not without its distortions and disfigurations.

I remember when Bryant Gumbel, then one of the biggest stars in morning network television, decided to take his show to Africa. There was much coverage of the event in the media. Though no fan of talk-show TV, I was infected by all the excitement—and decided to tune in. On a continent with numerous studios, Gumbel chose to broadcast from an open park, with animals prancing in the background. I hazard that he didn't mean to, but he reinforced the idea that animals were inescapable in the African landscape. They were, in fact, the dominant presences, a sort of synecdoche for the entire continent.

If Gumbel would choose to project Africa via the lens of animals, imagine the temptation for people who have even less information—and much less of a stake in the matter. One day, I arrived at Union Station, Hartford, to pick up my brother-in-law who was visiting from Nigeria and was supposed to come in on an Amtrak train. On finding out that his train was running thirty minutes late, I ducked into a nearby bar to have a beer while I waited. Soon two women walked in and took the stools nearest to me. They ordered drinks and instantly carried on a conversation in a loud voice, interspersed with carefree laughter that accentuated the impression that they were already inebriated. I feigned interest only in my drink but stole glances at them.

"Hi, honey, how you doing?" one of them addressed me. I had been too late to avert my gaze.

"Fine, and you?"

"We're having a great time," she said. Then she informed me that it was her companion's birthday.

"Oh, happy birthday," I said.

"Thanks, honey," the birthday celebrant replied. Then she added, "Where you from, sweetie? You have a cute accent. I just love it."

"From West Hartford," I said. "So do you. And I really love your accent."

"Me?" she asked, momentarily confused. "I don't have an accent. I was born here." With her forefinger she pointed down.

"I don't believe it. Right *here*?" I asked.

"I kid you not, honey."

"You were born right in this bar?"

She raised her head, and her laughter pierced the air. "You got a great sense of humor. No, I mean I was born and raised here, in Connecticut. Lived here all my life."

"That explains your accent," I insisted.

She laughed again. "You're too funny, honey. So, tell me for real, where you from?"

"I told you: West Hartford."

"I mean originally."

"I originally just came from there," I insisted, oddly enjoying the exchanges.

"You gotta be from Jamaica," her friend chimed in.

"Wrong; from Nigeria," I offered, sensing it was time to run back to the train station.

"Gotta be near Jamaica, though," suggested the birthday woman.

I stood up from the stool. "It's in Africa," I explained. "West Africa."

At the answer, her friend seemed to perk up. "You're from Africa, so what are you doing here, honey?" she asked, a touch of rebuke and pity in her tone. "If I was born in Africa, I would never leave. I love nature. Jungles, animals, I love it all."

"You like jungles and animals?" I asked.

"Believe me, honey."

"Then I'd suggest you move to Vermont," I said, hurrying away, the echo of their laughter rushing after me.

In the years since that whole phantasm of Africans riding on the backs of crocodiles, I have had fewer and fewer encounters with Americans ready to digest the most outlandish tales about

Africa and Africans. The Internet, with its one-click-away digest of news from anywhere on the globe, has made it harder to meet the likes of Chris or the two women at the Hartford bar. Innocence about Africa—or a species of ignorance around the continent and its diverse cultures—has yielded place, I must hope, to a deeper awareness. More and more American universities have established study-abroad programs in African countries, and large numbers of American students take classes in or on Africa—and often with African scholars.

For sure, there has been enough progress to permit the crocodile a well-deserved retirement from its commuter business. Even so, Africa remains in the imagination of some Americans a vortex of disease, an area of vestigial darkness and residual mystery.

WILL EDIT FOR FOOD

In mid-January 1992, *African Commentary*, the project that had brought me to America, died a sudden death. I have never had a claim to clairvoyance, but the magazine's demise was, for me, long foreseen.

From the outset, indeed twenty-four hours after my arrival in the United States, I developed the sneaking sense that the publication was fated for a fiasco. The name of the malaise, to be sure, was lack of cash.

Most of the magazine's board members were Nigerian academics in the United States. It'd be overstating it to say they were impecunious, but the reality was that most of them had little discretionary income. It meant that their financial investment in the publication ranged from a couple of thousand to thirty thousand dollars. And the cash was invested a little bit at a time, over a period of three years.

For many, the investment represented a significant bunch of change. They tried heroically—in my estimation, at least—to keep the magazine afloat. It just happened that they were using a few thousand dollars to prosecute a dream that demanded millions.

In fact, one or two of the magazine's board members put in nary a cent, instead lending intellectual capital. Intellectual capital was good. A little bit of cash would have been, I daresay, rather better.

African Commentary hardly had a fighting chance. A typical American magazine of comparable ambition would have a start-off budget in excess of five million dollars. Even so, a good number of those publications were still susceptible to high mortality rates. The magazine I edited never had a smidgen of that. To illustrate: the day after my arrival in the United States, Bart Nnaji, who served as the magazine's president and CEO, told me that *African Commentary* had only eleven thousand dollars in the bank. The dire implication was not lost on me: the magazine did not command enough cash even to pay one-third of my annual salary. For most of its checkered existence, even at the best of times, *African Commentary* could not count on five thousand dollars in its bank account.

The cash crunch translated into unceasing ordeals for me and the other staff. Some days I would arrive at the magazine's office at 29 Pray Street, Amherst, to dead phones—our service cut because the company had failed to pay its phone bill. Other times, there would be no electric power in the office, for the same reason. We made only fitful payments to our correspondents in different parts of the world. I had the painful, humiliating burden of inventing excuses for our delinquency. I was caught between the demands of brutal honesty about the state of our finances and offering garnished accounts—a tad too rosy, at times. I found a balance between portrayal of our difficulties and striking the right note of optimism to keep the correspondents from abandoning the magazine. Those we commissioned to write features, opinions, and reports were hardly ever paid.

It wore on me. Indeed, the magazine's financial woes brought the staff and me severe emotional and material suffering. I arrived at work one morning and saw the secretary in tears. She was a young woman in her early twenties, a recent graduate. The job with the magazine was her first employment after graduation.

"What's the matter?" I asked.

She covered her face and continued to sob, her body shaking. All I could do was mutter a string of phrases. *I'm sorry. Are you sick? Can I help you with anything? Do you need to go home?* To all my questions, she shook her head, but said no word. Then after a few minutes, she drew a deep breath, exhaled, and wiped tears with the back of her hand.

Only then, in a quaky voice, did she explain that she had had a disquieting phone conversation with a man who had written a piece for the magazine but had not received his fees. In fact, it was less a conversation than a verbal smacking. The writer had phoned and asked for me. When she explained that I wasn't in yet, the man had gone berserk. Suspecting her of shielding me from his fury, he had unleashed a flurry of curses on her. Then the writer-antagonist, who was based in New York, reminded her that he knew where we were. And he threatened to show up at our office and "kick all the asses I find there!"

"I'm so sorry for my reaction," the secretary said after telling me why she had been so upset.

"Not at all. I apologize that you had to go through this," I said.

I could not blame the irate writer. In fact, he and I had had several conversations over his pay. Each time he called, I apologized for the delay in paying him. I then explained our financial hardship. In turn, he told me that a huge chunk of his income came from his freelance journalism. "I can't pay my bills if I don't get paid for work," he'd say. I sympathized with his situation, I would assure him; then I'd promise to ensure he got paid within a week.

Not once did I mean my promise as deception—no. Each promise was made in earnest, driven by hope. I continually, stubbornly, hoped we would find money: enough to pay him, other contributors, our correspondents, and me. Yet, another week would pass, with no funds in sight. He'd call again, and we would go over the same ground, ending with the inevitable promise to pay—in a week.

I quietly acknowledged that my string of unredeemed promises had tried the writer's patience, brought him to the edge. I couldn't take umbrage at a man who, week after week, had bought the wishy-washy diet of hope I sold. Only I wished he had saved his fury until he had me on the phone, instead of lashing out at the magazine's innocent secretary.

There was little I could do to change the state of affairs at the office. The most I could do—which I realized, thanks to the vision and can-do spirit of the staff—was produce a fantastic magazine. *African Commentary* consistently received rave reviews. *Utne Reader* and *Library Journal* named it one of the best new publications of 1989. It received positive critical notice from National Public Radio (in an interview with publisher Chinua Achebe), *USA Today*, and the *Detroit Free Press*, among others. After each issue came a rain of letters to the editor commending the magazine's rich content.

Editorially, the publication was excellent. The trouble was that the whole magazine had been built on a shaky foundation, simple. Nnaji and Achebe and the magazine's other founders had undoubtedly conceived a noble idea, but they had also miscalculated the funding.

I felt particularly sorry for Nnaji. He was saddled with the impossible task of running a magazine with a pittance of funds. It was more than a full-time job, since there was always some fire to put out. He spent a lot of time at the magazine's office, ever busy at everyday tasks. Much of his time was taken up with cajoling our creditors—printers as well as phone and power companies, among them—to accept piecemeal, often minuscule, payment.

I often marveled at what he was able to accomplish, especially considering that he was also a first-class scientist and researcher. His robotics lab at the University of Massachusetts received substantial grants from General Electric and the National Science Foundation, among others.

Despite the magazine's paltry budget, Nnaji knew full well that the company ran the risk of inviting costly lawsuits if the American staff was not paid. His priority was to stretch what little funds he had to ensure that payroll was covered. In spite of his best efforts, twice or thrice, the paychecks bounced. Whenever that happened, he had to summon his best crisis-handling skills. He would show up at the office to offer explanations and apologies to the usually irate staff. On one occasion, I watched with awe and sadness as the magazine's production editor, an enterprising, cut-to-the-chase African American woman, dressed Nnaji down.

"I've got bills to pay, so I won't take it if my check bounces. Make sure it doesn't ever happen again, ever. If it does, you'll hear from my attorney."

A meek, chastened Nnaji promised it would never happen again.

For me, fresh from Nigeria, it was an illuminating experience. Two of the three publishers I had worked for in Nigeria paid their staff if and when it pleased them. Sometimes, my fellow workers and I were owed arrears of several months, even as the proprietors junketed around the world in the first-class cabin of major airlines. When we complained about unpaid salaries, we did so in hushed tones, in conspiratorial whispers—behind the back of the nonchalant, callous, delinquent employers.

Even though I sympathized with Nnaji—aware of the great sacrifice he made to keep a poorly funded magazine alive, if on life support—I found the workers' assertive demands on their pay rather refreshing.

Not that the culture of worker assertiveness helped my situation. I had it worse than the rest of the employees. In fact, I was given a variant of the Nigerian treatment.

As I stated, Nnaji did whatever he had to do—sometimes borrowing from his personal account—to ensure that the American staff got paid. The fear of litigation was constantly at the back of his mind, propelling him. But he could safely bet that I would not sue the magazine. He knew that, being new to America, I didn't know my way around labor laws and the whole business of retaining an attorney. I was an unlikely litigious threat. Beyond that, he must have figured that, as a product of a cultural ethos that valued forbearance, a culture that prized deference to "elders," I would be extremely reluctant to initiate a lawsuit against an employer whose board was chaired by Chinua Achebe, not only an eminent novelist but also an—arguably *the*—Igbo cultural icon.

Since the magazine was cash strapped, Nnaji reckoned that he could get away with paying a skimpy fraction of my salary or even skipping my salary altogether when there was not enough money to go round. The weeks when I was not paid at all, Nnaji would drive me to the Stop & Shop and stock me up with cereals, milk, rice, black-eye peas, chicken, beef, some fruits. "At least you should have food to eat," he would say to me.

My situation reminded me of those vagrants who haunt American street corners, a cardboard sign held aloft, inscribed with the plaintive proclamation WILL WORK FOR FOOD. I was editing a widely acclaimed international magazine—and I was working, week after week, for groceries!

Owed months of salary at a time—or paid only a fraction of what was due me—I was often delinquent in my rent payments. The rental company took to sending me eviction notices. Each time. I received an eviction warning, I made a torrent of desperate calls to friends and some members of the magazine's board. I felt disheartened to have to narrate my woes, especially to the same people whose failure to pay my salary had put me in the humiliating position of begging for rent money.

My pleas always yielded sympathetic responses. Friends and members of the magazine's board would pitch in various sums, anything from fifty dollars to two hundred dollars. Thanks to these benefactors, I was able, each month, to pay my rent. As I depended on the goodwill of donors, my rent, as a rule, was paid awfully late. No sooner did I pay one month's rent than the next month's rent fell due. I became an accumulator of eviction notices.

Oddly enough, my deeper concern was that I did not have the means to send school fees for my youngest brother and two cousins, who were at different universities. I was also worried that I could offer no financial support to my parents. How to meet those obligations kept me awake at night, lent an ache to my solitary moments. The last thing I wanted was for my parents to discover that things were not going well for me in America, that I was having a difficult time. If they knew, they'd agonize too much over me; they would suffer a lot on my account.

I had to come up with ploys to deflect their attention, leave the impression that I was doing well. Sometimes, I would take donations for my rent but send the cash to Nigeria for school-related fees. Other times, I would borrow from friends in order to send some money to my parents for their upkeep. When I spoke to them on the phone, I made a point of sounding upbeat.

All that borrowing and the staging of well-being devastated my ego. When I didn't have food, I would time my visits to friends' homes to improve my odds of getting a free meal. Even though I enjoyed the company of friends, I often chose to play recluse out of economic reason. When I was out, I made excuses when friends asked that I meet them at one bar or another in Amherst, Northampton, or Hadley. I cooked for my dates to avoid the expense of taking them to restaurants. A friend, Lloyd Thomas, helped me buy my first car in America, a Toyota Starlet, for two hundred dollars. Sometimes I had to park the car because I was late paying my automobile insurance fee, and coverage was removed.

The strain of financial hardship and other odds notwithstanding, I continued to work strenuously at the publication. I was fortunate that the rest of the staff shared my spirit. Somehow I hoped that some investor with deep pockets would take notice of the magazine and bring in the capital that would enable the publication to soar and achieve its potential.

I had also hoped that Achebe would use his wide contacts to entice investors. However, he appeared too engrossed in his literary activities to do more than contribute an occasional essay to the pages of the magazine. On several occasions, Nnaji and I would telephone him in Nigeria to report the dire state of the company. He would listen patiently and then ask that we send a courier message detailing the magazine's immediate and long-term investment needs. We would do so, but he never found time to do much about it. He was always on the move, drawn to speaking engagements and literary conferences in different parts of the world. Those demands apparently left him little time for the magazine; in fact, they seemed to sideline the needs of the publication.

The magazine's investment fortunes showed no signs of improving. Yet, Nnaji, the Jamaican novelist Ekwueme Michael Thelwell, and I persevered in searching for ways to save the floundering publication. A veteran of the civil rights movement, close to the fiery revolutionary crusader Stokely Carmichael (aka Kwame Ture), Thelwell was one of the staunchest champions of the magazine. He not only wrote some of the finest pieces in the publication, he also spread word about it to his numerous contacts from the civil rights movement. A great admirer of Achebe's literary work and cultural capital, the Jamaican-born writer was determined that the magazine not collapse. Achebe also admired him, bestowing on him the Igbo name Ekwueme—"one who lives up to his word."

One day, Bill Cosby, who was then at the height of his powers as an entertainer, came to town to give a talk at the University of Massachusetts, his alma mater. Thelwell asked the university's chancellor to arrange a brief private meeting between the comedian and Nnaji, Thelwell, and me. Our goal was to persuade Cosby to invest in the magazine. But we were wary of a too-direct proposal, which, we feared, carried the risk of rejection. We were going to adopt an indirect, even circuitous, strategy.

We gave Cosby copies of *African Commentary* as well as a copy of Achebe's book of essays, *Hopes and Impediments*, which had just been released. We then invited him to become one of the magazine's columnists. He gently declined, citing his hectic schedule. Next, we proposed doing a cover on him. Again, he turned us down. He insisted that such a cover would serve little or no purpose.

What he said next took our breaths away. "Gentlemen," he said, his large eyes sweeping our faces, "let me tell you how best I can be of help. I can invest in the magazine."

We were swept, without warning, into an exultant state. It was all we could do to keep from breaking into laughter or wild applause. It all seemed a rhetorical ambush, worthy of a man rather familiar with the kind of sinuous path we were taking to arrive at our main point—a request for investment. We did our best to keep our voices controlled as we expressed our gratitude.

Cosby wrote out the name and address of his investment company and asked us to forward a formal proposal to the firm. We did as he asked. Close to two weeks later, we received a response. Cosby would not be investing after all, the firm wrote. We had felt buoyant after meeting with Cosby; now, with the rejection letter in hand, we came crashing down, mercilessly, on hard ground.

Nnaji and I made other efforts to find investors. The erudite Ghanaian writer Kofi Awoonor, who was then his country's ambassador and permanent representative at the United Nations, tried to broker an investment deal with a group of Haitians, most of them doctors, based in New York City. They appeared interested in bringing in close to a half-million dollars in exchange for a significant stake in *African Commentary*. They also demanded that Achebe cede one of his two posts—as chairman of the board and publisher—to enable them to nominate one of their number to occupy it. Achebe was not enamored of the idea. The possibility of the Haitian group's investment fizzled out.

Meanwhile, the magazine's debt mounted. Nnaji found it more difficult to find the money to pay salaries. My finances became even more pitiful, my bank account parched. Week after week, I didn't know whether I would be paid a fraction of my salary or Nnaji would drive me to a store and buy me groceries in lieu of payment.

I became an even-more-desperate borrower. From time to time, I was commissioned by *Emerge* magazine to write a piece on some African country or issue. Whenever I received any funds, whether borrowed or earned from journalistic work, I sent much of it home. I was anxious to sustain my parents in the impression that my personal and professional lives had few wrinkles.

But my relationship with some of our correspondents continued to deteriorate. One of them, Sam Nwanuforo, then a graduate student at Leicester University, met Achebe in London where the novelist delivered the Southbank Lecture. Even though we were friends and I had confided in him about the magazine's financial troubles, he sent me an angry letter through Achebe in which he accused me of willfully refusing to pay him. According to him, Achebe had denied that the magazine had financial problems and had asked him to submit a list of what he needed to continue to do his work. I was mystified, for Achebe knew quite well that our financial condition was wretched. The publisher-novelist had made a stop at the magazine's office the day he was leaving for London—and our electricity had been disconnected because we hadn't paid the utility firm. Nwanuforo's letter strained our friendship. It would be several years before we spoke again during my visit to the United Kingdom.

A few correspondents rebelled by balking at new assignments. I was in a helpless situation. I knew that, if I couldn't wring assignments out of them, then the magazine was in the throes of death.

In the midst of the worsening crisis, we held a critical board meeting at which Achebe was absent. When Nnaji proposed that we

aggressively look for new outside investors, one of the members—
a classmate of Achebe's at university—countered that the novelist's
permission was needed since he owned the magazine. At this point
Nnaji disclosed that he, not the novelist, had come up with the original idea for the magazine. A few days after the meeting, he sent each
board member a written account of the publication's provenance.

That innocuous-seeming move proved fatal for the magazine.
The next time the board met, in January 1992, with Achebe present, the members were riven in half over the argument of who
founded the magazine. Neither faction was willing to invest more
funds in a project that had soaked up so much of some members'
hard-earned savings but still needed a lot more money—in fact, a
few million dollars.

The feud became intractable. A day after the heated board meeting of January 1992, Nnaji faxed his letter of resignation to fellow
board members. With him gone, the doleful sign was writ even
more large for me: there could no longer be any *African Commentary*
to speak of, not even in the tottering sense that it had operated for
more than three years.

I handed in my own letter of resignation. The letter brimmed
with resentment and outrage. I had come to America to set up a
magazine that held great promise. And that lofty potential had
been torpedoed as much by the clash of egos as by the lack of cash.

Achebe called an emergency meeting at his home on the campus
of Bard College in Annandale-on-Hudson in upstate New York. I
was not invited. The sole item on the agenda: the announcement
of his resignation.

I had come to America filled with hope and great expectations
for the magazine. I had sacrificed a lot, as had most board members, and it had all come to nought. An entire dream lay in a waste.
One road had closed suddenly, even if with considerable augury,
and I couldn't yet see any other road opening up.

I was confused and incensed and at the edge of despair.

LYING TO BE A WRITER

The demise of *African Commentary* early in 1992 cast me in a thick emotional fog. I was too devastated to see beyond the pain of the moment, too distraught to imagine the prospect of a path beyond the profound disillusion that was my reality. In many ways, I was a man adrift, unsure of what would come next; uncertain, even, that there was something like a future, a "next."

My days were filled with endless dawdling, going in and out of used bookstores, seeking some kind of rejuvenation of spirits, some manner of comfort. It was entirely futile. I would open a book and gaze absentmindedly at its words, lifeless things strewn on the page, and then shut the book in pained resignation. Nothing spoke to me anymore, least of all books. Even so, with little else to engage me, I made a fetish of visiting dust-flecked used bookstores.

One day, I stepped out of a bookstore and saw the prizewinning writer John Edgar Wideman. He'd been a columnist for *African Commentary* and was quite close to Ekwueme Michael Thelwell. He and I exchanged greetings and made small talk. Then he remarked, "I'm sorry the magazine's folded. It was very much needed."

I agreed.

"A sad, sad loss," he said. Then he asked: "So now that the magazine's ceased, what do you plan to do?"

My mind ran this way and that, seeking some answer that would make a semblance of sense, some idea that would represent a coherent pattern between my immediate past as editor of an international magazine and the trajectory of a future, dimly glimpsed.

"I don't know," I finally said. It was a terse answer, the most honest I could manage.

Wideman looked me intensely in the eye. "You're working on a novel, right?"

I wasn't writing a novel. But Wideman's tone suggested a confidence, an unmistakable certitude, that I was a budding novelist. How long did he hold me in that withering gaze, as if double daring me to declare I was *not* writing a novel? I feared that, should I state the truth, the man would never ever talk to me any more.

"Yes," I answered, certain there was no other choice.

Wideman's eyes softened, his expression became calm, unworried, as if my response had righted the day. "I've talked to Michael [Ekwueme Thelwell] about helping out. Why not get me fifteen to twenty pages of your manuscript—and let's see if we can get you into the MFA program at UMass."

The conversation with Wideman—culminating in my lie about writing a novel—was eerie, a near reprise of an earlier encounter in Nigeria.

That earlier event happened in 1988, the same year I relocated to the United States. I had boarded a Nigeria Airways domestic flight flying from Lagos to Enugu. Soon after, a lanky man walked in, his air of privilege unmistakable, and sat in the seat next to mine. I recognized him as Dillibe Onyeama, the author of a widely popular, edgy memoir, *Nigger at Eton*. A product of one of the best public schools in Britain, he was the scion of a legal luminary, Justice Daddy Onyeama, who served on the International Court of Justice at The Hague. I had heard him speak on TV with a perfect English elocution.

I nodded in his direction but felt too excited to utter a word. I had met few writers at close quarters, and anybody who'd written a book held an allure of magic. But shortly after the plane lifted into the air, I found my voice.

"I am a fan of yours," I said in a shaky voice.

"Lovely," he said with English reserve, but breaking into a smile.

I let a moment pass, and then announced that I was a journalist.

"What paper?" he asked, his tone revealing more interest than I expected.

"*African Guardian.* A weekly magazine."

"Of course," he said with palpable interest. "What's your name?"

I told him my name. His smile widened. He told me that he knew and enjoyed my work.

I thanked him and lifted a book halfway to my face, pretending to read. In reality, I was still hoisted on a crest of excitement. Here was a bona fide writer, and one who spoke English as proficiently as the very originators of the language, and he knew who I was, down to being familiar with my writing. A few minutes later, from the corner of my eye, I caught the writer looking at me.

"You must be writing a novel, right?" he asked.

"Yes," I said, like a programmed machine, before I had had time to think.

"Do submit it to Delta," he said. He had just set up the publishing company in Enugu.

I pretended to turn once again to the book, to discourage him from probing about my so-called novel. Moments later, I felt I could speak with calmness.

"How did you figure out I was writing a novel?" I asked.

"Oh, your writing style. Whenever I read you in the magazine, you have that novelistic style."

Slowly, unobtrusively, I took a deep breath.

I returned to Lagos and set to writing what I imagined was a novel. It was the story of a university-age Yoruba girl disinherited by her rich father after she reveals her love for an Igbo man from a wretched background. Then, once the man graduates as an accountant and gets a lucrative corporate job, he ditches her—for an Igbo bride. The Yoruba woman, rejected by her father and jilted by the man she loves, is bereft and heartbroken. In her loneliness, she turns to her paternal grandmother, the only person still willing to open her arms in a gesture of unconditional love.

I wrote the manuscript in longhand, on foolscap sheets. In less than two months, I was done. I handed it to one of the typists at the magazine to type it for me, for a fee. He had not finished when Achebe invited me to the United States to edit *African Commentary*.

A week or two after my arrival in the United States, I realized—in a hard, sobering way—that I had not written a novel. At best, I had taken what should have been a short story and stretched and stretched it to answer to the name: "novel." You want to know how I figured that out? Let me tell you.

In Nigeria—in the late 1980s—few, if any, bookstores would allow a wandering customer to thumb through the pages of a book for more than a few seconds. Books belonged on shelves. Browsing customers could look at the book-lined shelves as long as they wished, but they were not permitted to pull out a book unless they meant to pay for it. If a customer lingered over a book, the salesperson was bound to order, often brusquely, "If you're buying, buy; if you're not, put it down!"

Then, arriving in America, I beheld the wonder of the bookstore equipped with couches. It was hard to believe that I could pull out several magazines and books, lower myself in a couch or comfortable chair, and read to my heart's content. And I could do this day after day, and no staff of the store was going to give me an evil eye much less order me to buy the book or magazine already—or put it back. Americans had taught me the saying, "There's no free lunch." I was more than pleased to take free reading!

Many an evening, I went to one or another of the bookstores in Amherst. I would scan through the fiction section and pull out novels and other texts whose titles caught my fancy. I remember harvesting books by Gabriel Garcia Marquez and Wideman and Toni Morrison and Carlos Fuentes and Andre Brink and some ancient greats like Sophocles and Homer. Then I'd find a place to sit and start reading them. As I read, I had this awakening: the manuscript I had finished in Nigeria was nowhere near the quality of writing and dramatic complexity of these novels.

A year later, I had my first opportunity to visit Nigeria. The typist handed me a bundle, both the handwritten and typed versions of my ostensible novel. In a flash, gripped by an access of rage I would later regret, I tore it all to shreds.

Four years later after my conversation with Onyeama, John Edgar Wideman would echo the Nigerian writer's question. Once again, I was left no choice but to lie. And, having lied, I had to start (again) writing a novel.

That night, I began to scribble. I wrote with a measure of desperation commensurate with what was at stake. I had no subject, but I chose a madman to be at the center of the narrative, as my protagonist.

Ever since my teenage years, the insane had fascinated me. What was their history? When did they turn mad, and how? Was there some symmetry and logic to their thoughts and actions?

Growing up, I had known several madmen and -women. I used to spend long hours trailing them, observing their idiosyncrasies, eavesdropping on their utterances. Sometimes, I would speak to them, try to coax them into a conversation.

There was the reedy woman, Ugoada, who daily traversed a road that cut my secondary school in two. She would often stake out a position outside the school's kitchen, bowl in hand. She would plant herself there until one of the kitchen staff gave her two or three scoops of *akamu*, a hot porridge made from ground fermented corn.

There was "World Man," distinguished by his bloodshot eyes,

dreadlock hair, and scholar's goatee. He walked with a limp and wore his shirts unbuttoned, so that they fluttered when the breeze blew. He haunted a busy junction in my hometown, Amawbia. He would weave through gaps between cars trapped in traffic. Then, pausing beside a driver, he'd hold out a hand and speak his signature phrase: *"Oko* [buddy], give me money." It was said of him that he'd been a bright student but had smoked something illicit that fouled up his brain.

There was another madman whose right foot was missing two toes. He always wore shorts as he trolled homes, including the postmaster's quarters where we lived, asking for money and food. He declared himself to be Jesus and promised salvation to those who gave him money. He loved the thrill of a moving vehicle. Once he'd collected some money, he would hop into a commuter vehicle. He would pay for the terminal destination in either direction, either Onitsha to the west or Enugu to the east. *"Uto motor, uto ebe!"* he'd exclaim as he settled in a bus ("The sweetness of a car ride, sweet indeed!").

I was going to make the mad people I knew grist for my would-be fiction. I was going to attempt to imagine not only their language but also the inner landscape of their minds. I had confirmed Wideman in his impression that I was working on a novel, and I had to put up. I wrote, resolved to capture the churning, chaotic, unpredictable mind of a madman.

Each step of the way, the writing was dogged by self-doubt, hampered by a sense that it would all end in futility. I couldn't tell whether what I was setting down resembled fiction in any form. All I could go on was the fact that I had read voraciously at that point in my life. And, in particular, I had read a lot of novels, from different parts of the world, on different subject matters, in different styles, different periods. Yet, that experience, I realized, was no guarantee that I could write a novel. At best, it meant I was able to say which writers and styles I liked, which I didn't. Yet, if one was able to make aesthetic judgments as a reader, it did not follow that one could write a novel. Not even one patterned on one's favorite style.

Were the circumstance different, perhaps doubt would have crippled my endeavor. But the stakes were too high. I could afford to give Wideman some weird draft he would not recognize as fiction; but I didn't have the option of handing him nothing. He and I lived in Amherst, and there were good odds we'd run into each other again. How would I explain not showing him a section of my manuscript when he had said he might help get me into UMass's MFA program?

Over the weekend, my labor and ardor yielded twenty-three typed pages. I dropped off the harvest at Wideman's office at Bartlett Hall, University of Massachusetts. Two days later, he rang me.

"I found your writing fascinating," he said. "It reminded me of the fiction of Ngũgĩ wa Thiong'o."

I was not only relieved that I hadn't produced work that made a fool of myself; I was, in fact, flattered. The Kenyan writer Ngũgĩ wa Thiong'o was one of my favorite novelists of all time. And I admired his social commitment, his advocacy for the peasants and poor of his country, an activism that earned him censorship, detention, and exile from his native country.

Wideman and his friend Michael Thelwell arranged for me to take the Graduate Records Examinations (GRE). And then, true to his promise, Wideman found funds to enable me to register for the MFA degree. Unable to secure my transcripts from Nigeria, I could not register until the next academic year, 1993.

Years later, Ngũgĩ and I were together in Nairobi, Kenya, to attend the Kwani Literary Festival. Over breakfast, I told him how I had lied to become a writer. He laughed for a long time. And then he told me that he, too, had done something similar.

As a student at Makerere University in Uganda, he had one day

chanced upon a senior student who was the editor of the university's literary journal. The editor was something of a star on campus,
especially among students in the humanities. Ngũgĩ said he had
very much wanted to hold a conversation with the man but wanted
for a handle, a topic that would make the editor pause and deign
to talk.

On an impulse, he told the man he'd written a short story.
He feared the man would brush him off and continue on his way.
Instead, the editor paused, flashed a smile, and asked him to sub-
mit the story.

Ngũgĩ rushed off to his hostel and began writing what became
his first story—and the beginning of an illustrious literary career.

Once I enrolled in the MFA program, the manuscript I had
handed to Wideman began to mutate. Its working title changed
from *Dry Dreams* to *Spikes of Rain* and, finally, to *Arrows of Rain*.
After writing close to sixty pages in the voice of a madman, I became
scared about the health of my own mind. I decided to write, not
about a madman as such, but about a protagonist who, on the exte-
rior, looks the part, but, on closer scrutiny, as the dramatic events
unfold, reveals himself as frighteningly sane.

I treasure telling audiences, especially of aspirant writers, how
a lie offered me a path to a vocation as a writer. I always end by
underscoring the moral of the story: Lie about being a writer, if you
have to, but have the courage, grit, and stamina to turn that lie on
its head, make it spell truth.

WRITING, READING, FOOD, SOME ASS KICKING

The MFA program at the University of Massachusetts opened my eyes to new ways of growing as a writer. Many writers and scholars quibble about whether writing programs advance or hamper creative work. In my case, I learned a lot, about reading and writing and about people, in the classroom—and outside of it.

When I look back on that time, I think of one word: "banquet." I had never had an experience that remotely resembled a writing workshop. Each session sustained the impression that one was at a banquet. Stories were at the center of the communion, but food and drinks were also inseparable parts of the ritual.

The literary parts of the banquets were hardly ever smooth, hitch-free affairs. Every now and then, the discussions got contentious, stories received bruising comments, tempers flared, and the atmosphere became charged. But even those difficult shifts seemed to me indispensable and necessary. They helped keep the literary banquets exciting, served as payoffs for those moments when everything was in sync, no voices were raised, nobody colored red or choked up, no nerves got tested.

I had read a fair number of novels, short stories, and plays, but I went into the writing program with some pretty bad writing manners. I was a consummate overwriter, a splurger on sentences. I never could resist the temptation to write five sentences when one would do. As a reader, I liked fiction and poetry that incorporated ellipses and other forms of gaps, works that invited me to be an active reader, indeed challenged me to be a cocreator of meaning. Yet, I wrote in a manner that spelled out too much, handed the reader everything, if I could manage it. In workshops, I began to learn that less was often more, that narrative economy could be a mark of genius, and discerning when and how to hold back could translate into offering your reader whole new universes to discover, explore, be enchanted by, play in.

Despite my experience as a reader, I hadn't divined how dialogue worked in fiction. I took fiction, which can be a serious matter, *too* seriously, almost like a grave, joyless thing. The characters in the first drafts I offered for workshop spoke like philosophers. It was just that their speech was often that—speech. They spoke in a ponderous manner, their diction appropriate to a gathering of book people who had forgotten how to speak and connect like humans. I said my characters spoke like philosophers; I lied. They spoke like bad imitators of what bad philosophers might sound like—if such a breed existed. They used words like "profound" and "verify" and "incumbent" (as in "It's incumbent upon you") and "expatiate" and "egregious" and "phantasmagoria."

Therein lay my biggest challenge as a student of fiction. I had to learn how to "normalize" (I didn't want to use the word "naturalize") my characters' conversations. It took me most of the three years in the MFA program to finally figure it out. I wrote and rewrote dialogue, as if my writing life depended on mastering that technology, which it did. I became a collector of conversations. Wherever I was—on a bus, in a train, in a restaurant, on campus, at a bar—I eavesdropped on people's conversations. In time, dialogue became my suit.

For me, it was extraordinary to take workshops with writers as varied in their style of writing and teaching as John Edgar

Wideman, Jay Neugeboren, George Cuomo, and the Hungarian émigré Tamas Aczel. Wideman was the star of the department, and his workshops were the first to fill. His classroom style was quietly mesmeric. A former college basketball player, he still retained a tall, spare physique. As he spoke, he moved his hands, his long fingers spread apart, molding invisible shapes in the air. It was as if he were conducting his own speech. His ethic eschewed prescriptiveness. Instead, he would focus on the "spirit" of the story. Using a multiplex vocabulary, drawn from psychology, philosophy, history, popular culture, and myth, he would ask a series of questions of or about a story. You emerged from his workshop with the sense of having undergone a quasi-spiritual immersion. He challenged you to think about fiction's fecund facility for slipping on different masks, touching and even changing us in predictable and unforeseen ways.

Neugeboren had a keen editorial nose. He was quick at sniffing out verbose, loopy, self-indulgent writing. In fact, he had this ability to sift through a page of a story and point to the two or three sentences that had done the job. He became the great tamer of my verbiage, the nurturer in me of a tighter register of language. When he didn't like a story, he was wont to speak candidly. Yet, as his handsome, youngish face seemed forever lit with a smile, his critical judgments never came across as mean-spirited.

As I remarked earlier, food was an important feature of my experience at UMass, a delectable companion to the cerebral part of the banquet. Each year, Wideman hosted a party at his home in Amherst. Neugeboren did the same, at his creaky home in Northampton.

Cuomo did not wait till the end of the school year to throw his own parties. Our workshop met at his home, tucked into the center of a salute of trees. Each session was a combo of culinary feast and literary excursion, as if he had discovered a potent ancient secret derived from juxtaposing food and fiction. For each workshop, he provided drinks—soda, beer, wine, even the occasional liquor. He also scheduled students to take turns bringing food. Most of my classmates would provide varieties of chips, cookies, vegetables, and dips. When it came my turn, I decided to (literally) spice things up. I made a spicy chicken and tomato sauce, a spicy black-eyed-pea porridge, and white rice. As they ate, my classmates sniffled, daubed at their teary eyes, and wiped their sweaty faces and heads. One of them, an Irish American, was so beset that he glowed deep crimson. When he was able to feel his tongue, he pronounced that it was the spiciest food he had ever let into his mouth. Everybody roared in laughter when I described the cuisine as delicious agony. Cuomo loved the food, particularly because of its heat index. He accepted my offer to keep what was left, which was sizable.

His workshop style was more laid-back and homier than the ones that came before and after. An architectural acumen seemed to be at the center of his perceptivity. Where Wideman searched out narrative spirits and Neugeboren took a scalpel to flabby language, Cuomo had an eye for design flaws in a story. His questions probed deep. He was the kind of teacher who wanted to know why you put this block *here*, placed that one *there*.

Cuomo and Tamas Aczel had a kinship, their fascination with the epicurean dimension of creativity. Food and drinks also featured in a fiction workshop I took with Aczel during the spring semester of 1993. What stood out for me was a humorous encounter with the teacher. It became one of several turning points in the evolution of my confidence as a writer.

Aczel's teaching style—in academic lingo, his pedagogy—was the first thing that got me hooked. By "style," I don't mean anything quite so high-minded, nothing to do with what scholars might call discursive practice, nothing that pertained to the way he deconstructed narratives or plumbed texts. No, I refer to something rather primal, basic.

At the professor's behest, our class met at the Lord Jeffery Inn, a regal restaurant that had long been a fixture in the center of Amherst.

There were twelve of us in Aczel's fiction workshop. We were as varied a group of writers and readers as could be found in any gathering of twelve scribblers. Yet, as the semester progressed, we coalesced into a close-knit group of writers and readers.

One reason for this was our shared passion. We were all deeply invested in the banquet of reading and writing—and, yes, eating and drinking, too. I'd suggest, however, that a far more important reason was Aczel himself. He was an understated but quietly magnetic presence, and he acted as the glue for our small creative community. There was an avuncular gravitas about the man. That gift enabled him to hold our idiosyncrasies in check and beseeched us to coalesce into a close-knit, cohesive tribe, a republic forged by letters.

I'd hazard that the ambience of the Lord Jeffery shaped the dynamics of the workshop. At each weekly workshop session, Aczel picked up the bill for our drinks: beer, wine, spirits, juice, and soda. Sometimes, his generosity on an expansive scale, he also paid for hors d'oeuvres. We'd eat and drink as we responded to our peers' short stories or excerpts from novels or grappled with some question of craft or broad issue of literary practice that Aczel would provoke.

The experience of being in Aczel's workshop set my conviction that few other sensations could trigger imaginative flights and dispose the mind to creative contemplation better than the sight and fragrance of food—and the seductive power of beverage on the tongue.

Aczel was in physique rather short and smallish, but he managed to project a patrician carriage. His face suggested erudition and aristocratic bearing, the kind of features that would be a portrait artist's delight. It was stamped by time, so that he looked older than his seventy years. Yet, time did not mar as much as it decorated him. An artist's impressionist rendition of his face would, most likely, include a pipe hanging from the lips, a wisp of smoke curved upward, slightly obscuring sharp, lively eyes, narrowed.

By the time I met him in 1993, Aczel, at seventy-one, was a year away from his death on April 18, 1994. He was hunched over, often walked with a cane, his gait slow. Sometimes he seemed lost in his long, dark winter coat. Yet, there was nothing deathly about his appearance or manners. He had a commanding presence, one that filled any space he entered.

He spoke an urbane English, in a deliberate, cultivated vein. His voice, clear and resonant, belied his age—or, more, his looks. And there was a faintly Oxonian quality to his enunciation, his speech shaped, doubtless, by the years he spent in the UK after breaking with the Communist rulers of his native Hungary in the late 1950s.

At our workshops, he spoke sparingly, as if words were the most dear of commodities, the overuse of which he considered unconscionable. Sometimes he offered broad comments on the story or novel excerpt we were critiquing. Sometimes he zeroed in on some technical detail. Sometimes he asked a question or a series of questions, nudging us to think about some aspect of a work. A man of prodigious intellect, he often mentioned some familiar or remote author or unknown or known text that a work under critique recalled for him.

His was the second workshop I ever took as an MFA student. I was still at the stage when I was in awe of my professors and tried to hang on to every word that came from their lips. Aczel happened to be a parsimonious speaker. For me, then, whatever he had to say seemed to have some weight to it, highly precious.

I became curious about him. I began to dig up bits and pieces about him. What I found must have been a concatenation of facts and fiction. It nevertheless transformed the man, in my eyes, into a legend. The crux of my findings was this: once upon a time, the man had been a towering figure in the literary circles of Communist Hungary. He'd won the highest state-sponsored accolades. In the end, he had become despondent about the Hungarian Communist regime, particularly the predations of its apparatchiks whose fealty was to their Soviet masters. He'd risked life and limb for a while as a dissident but ultimately fled to London. In the UK, he had found both love and a new space that conduced to the free roam of his imaginative spirit. Then, fed up with an intellectual atmosphere in Europe that sometimes flirted with or romanticized communism, he had made another flight, this time across the waters to the United States.

A year or two before I became his student, Aczel had published what proved to be his last novel, *The Hunt*. The work had appeared after a hiatus of close to a decade since the writer's previous novel, *Illuminations*.

I doubt that any of us in Aczel's workshop had read his books. Yet, I took it on faith that I was in the presence of a writer of immense consequence. In fact, my decision not to read his last book felt like a negative act of homage. It was a ploy to conserve my intuitive sense of the man's fame and greatness, lest the familiarity with the work leave me disappointed, disillusioned.

Aczel's act of defiance, his renunciation of political orthodoxy, struck a chord with me. As a fledgling MFA student, I wanted to get his response to my writing—the seed that became my first novel, *Arrows of Rain*. Close to the end of the first round of workshops, I offered two consecutive chapters of *Arrows* for a critique session.

I arrived at the Lord Jeffery in a mood split between mild excitement and anxiety. Before class started, I took healthy gulps of my Guinness draft to brace myself. Then, as was the custom, Aczel asked me to read a few paragraphs from my work. My classmates began to respond to it. Most of them liked it, others made suggestions for revisions, and one or two were no fans. Many of the comments bordered on my use of dialogue, too scripted and implausible. It was a typical day at the workshop. Only there was something awfully odd: Aczel did not utter a word. His silence left me unnerved.

Class ended, and I fully intended to make a swift escape, confused as hell.

"Okey," Aczel called out. His stentorian voice stopped me in my tracks. "I'd like you to come see me in my office."

"Okay," I managed, a lump caught in my throat.

A day or two later, I mustered the courage to knock on his door at Bartlett Hall.

"Come in," he beckoned.

His head was down when I walked in. He was reading something, the bridge of his glasses at the very tip of his nose. Without much raising his head, he lifted his eyes and gave me a quick wash of a look. Then, raising a hand, he gestured to a chair. I sat down at the very edge of the seat. He read for another two or three minutes, then scribbled a note in longhand. Finally, he looked up at me, removed his glasses, and regarded me with piercing eyes.

"Do you know why I asked you to come see me?"

I knew: my writing had thoroughly disappointed him. But I wasn't going to confess it. I wasn't about to compound my humiliation. So I said, "No."

"Well," he said, "of the stories we've looked at so far in class, yours strikes me as having a great potential to become a book. I want you to promise me you'll continue working on it until it becomes a book."

He regarded me with intense, curious eyes. I smiled awkwardly, still stressed out from thinking the worst.

"Do you promise?" he asked in a raised voice, a strident judge asking a parolee if he promised to resist the lure of recidivism.

"I do," I said.

"Of course you do! Otherwise I'd kick your ass!"

He roared with laughter. I laughed, too, out of relief. But something else had helped trigger my amusement. For I pictured the committee of at least two persons that it would take to accomplish an ass kicking by the writer. One person would have the task of lowering me close to the ground, the other the job of raising Aczel's leg to kick said ass, and then to return the leg to its original position.

⭐ ⭐ ⭐
A BRAND-NEW AMERICAN

On May 10, 1996, in a cavernous hall at the US District Court in Hartford, Connecticut, in the presence of a judge and a flag of the United States of America, I raised my right hand and, with solemnity, declared on oath my renunciation and abjuration of "all allegiance and fidelity to any foreign prince, potentate, state, or sovereignty of whom or which I have heretofore been a subject or citizen," and other words along the same lines, and, when I ended with the phrase "So help me God," the judge smiled expansively and welcomed me—and many other oath takers—as brand-new citizens of the American republic.

The event was deeply moving, in part because it was, for me, colored by paradox, some pain, even ambiguity. The moment's emotional fuel enabled me to travel back in memory to the thoughts and sensations that marked my early encounter with America.

Taking the oath, I recalled the day of my arrival in America, lugging one suitcase and loads of advice—remarkably from friends and relatives who knew little or nothing at all about America.

I had come to find it amusing that, thanks to the westerns that Hollywood long ago exported to the rest of the world, my relatives, like many other Nigerians, were confident that they knew what America was all about. And their dominant image of America was of mean streets where swashbucklers held sway, their guns drawn, ready to wreak havoc at the slightest provocation—or none at all. As far as some relatives of mine were concerned, America was some sort of concrete jungle, where the tough and mighty reigned, and arguments were settled—decisively won—by the man able to pull the faster *bam-bam*.

This image was not any more ludicrous than some Americans' impressions of Africa, including that example of a graduate student who believed my yarn about crocodiles ferrying Africans across the Atlantic to the shores of North America!

In 1996, I had lived eight years in America. I had come to forgive America all its sins against me—especially that chilly reception the day I first arrived, the blast of evil cold that left my jaws chattering, and that near arrest for bank robbery that had so terrified me. Better still: I had purged myself of the notion of being wronged—maliciously, even—by America.

Yet, those memories of injustice marked—in some ways marred—the beginning of my American rite of passage. Even so, neither America nor I was in a haste to demand a divorce. Instead, the romance blossomed, more strengthened than wrecked by its vicissitudes. The culmination came in 1996, in my adoption of American citizenship.

From the outset, inevitably, a sense of contrast had framed my American experiences. I had viewed America through my African sensibility; through it, I sifted, weighed, and evaluated the multitudinous impulses that were a part of my everyday experience in the United States. Looking back at any point, I could see that much that was painful, hilarious, humdrum, or illumining had happened between the day I came to America and the day I took up American citizenship.

In Nigeria, I was used to my apartment being invaded at will by friends. They would stay as long as they wished, sometimes several days at a time, and help themselves to what food I had as well as drinks. By contrast, my American friends made sure to phone before they called at my apartment. Sometimes they would telephone several days before.

Such American drama went apace. Everywhere I turned, America—Americans—intrigued me. I was amazed that people here would walk past one another without exchanging a word, rather like dumbstruck waifs. Back in Nigeria, none but the notoriously evil or socially maladjusted lacked for friends. I had come from a place where people shake hands a lot, even compulsively, sometimes with near strangers. Indeed, the Nigerian world I had been conversant with was one in which people lived and had their being, for the most part, in a communal space.

In America, I learned of something called personal space and of Americans' unshakable commitment to its preservation. It meant, among other things, that you did not intrude on your fellows without first obtaining their permission, without hatching out the terms of the intrusion.

For a while, I felt greatly astonished about personal space. I saw the idea as a plague, spelling the very doom of what it means to be human. Seen from the angle of my cultural background and experience, the idea of a zealously claimed personal space seemed pregnant with peril. It signaled isolation, disconnection, pain, and alienation.

No, my American friends assured me, personal space was a wonderful zone to inhabit. They explained it as an inviolable vantage point, sometimes as a bubble from which one could "get in tune" with oneself. It was all gobbledygook to me. The idea of getting in tune with oneself was akin to holding oneself in open conversation. Where I was born, such a quirk was associated with the insane.

I set out to wage a personal battle against personal space.

That battle was dramatized by an encounter with Kitty Axelson, one of my first American friends, our friendship clicking soon after she showed up one morning at my door and asked if I would consider writing for the *Valley Advocate*. Some weekends, she'd ask me to take part in a softball game she and her circle of friends and family played. She invited me to my first Thanksgiving dinner where I met even more of her friends and family. A gregarious person, I was always greedy for friends. Kitty was not just a friend; she also gave me the gift of numerous other friends.

Even though I esteemed her as a dear friend, Kitty had the (American) habit of ringing me to ask if she and her boyfriend could drop in at my apartment. Sometimes, she would give me as much as a three-day notice.

"You don't have to ask, Kitty," I would explain at each turn. "You and Hank are my friends. You should come to my door anytime you wish."

"But that would be rude," she'd insist.

"No. What's rude, actually, is to ask a friend's permission to visit him."

"But you may be in the middle of something," she'd persist.

"That's fine. If that's the case, you can exchange quick greetings and leave. And return at a later time."

She never could bring herself to go by my stipulation. One day, I decided to offer an emphatic illustration in how friends related. Without serving prior warning, I drove up to the home in the leafy, hilly woods of Leverett, Massachusetts. I rang their doorbell.

Kitty came to the door and seemed to do a double take. I held a steady smile, and she presently found her voice.

"Hi, Okey," she said, doing her best to work up a measure of warmth. She seemed to me painfully perplexed. "What a surprise. Come on in."

We sat in their kitchen that opened out to a grassy incline that led to a jagged, winding valley. Finally she asked, "Is everything okay?"

"Yes," I assured her. "This is how we do it in Nigeria. We just show up."

"Interesting," she said. But she spelled out that she still preferred to be given notice before a guest, even one who was a friend, showed up.

I left a bit dismayed but also educated. After the surprise visit to Kitty Axelson, I realized that I would have little chance of converting her—or other Americans—to conform to my cultural norms. I gave the matter much thought. Slowly, I came to concede that my ways were not better—they were, simply, different.

How I must have tried some of my American friends' patience. For my part, I found some Americans and their ways odd, bewildering, and, often, hilarious.

Almost every summer, my parents-in-law would visit from Nigeria and spend two or three months with my family and me in West Hartford, Connecticut. One day, a classmate in a graduate course at the University of Massachusetts Amherst asked how my weekend went.

"I drove my parents-in-law to JFK. They traveled back to Nigeria after visiting us for two and a half months."

Her jaw dropped, and she regarded me with a look that suggested I had been subjected to cruel and unusual punishment.

"Two and a half months with your in-laws?" she asked. "How could you stand it?"

"It was no problem," I explained. "I actually felt sad that they left. To have them around is like hosting my own parents."

"You like *your* parents that much?" she asked.

I burst out in loud laughter, alone; she had not tried to be funny.

AMERICANS' RELATIONSHIP WITH THEIR dogs and other pets both impressed me and tickled me silly. For a while, I wondered why there was such a fetish around pets, dogs above all. I don't believe I have figured it all out, but my observations have shaped my view of life in America. In a society where people are obsessed with personal space, dogs have come to serve as welcome, neo-human mediators of loneliness and solitude. In the late 1990s, for example, I became friends with Richie and Helen Salomon, who lived in my neighborhood in West Hartford, Connecticut. They were siblings, Richie older by two years, both of them more than eighty years old. Neither sibling ever married or had a child. For fifty-some years, they had lived together. In the time I knew them, their only regular companion was a dog they named, simply, Doggie. They doted on the dog. They talked about the dog's idiosyncrasies with the same indulgent tone parents might use in discussing a child.

Without Doggie, Richie and Helen's lives would have had no center, little salt, none of that healthy, vitalizing dose of disturbance that those whose lives are rich and fulfilling know, rue sometimes, but need. Remove Doggie and the elderly siblings' experience would have had little color to it, little depth. They would have had nothing, beyond themselves, to activate and engage that most human of faculties: an ability for empathetic feeling, a desire to take care of somebody, something other than the self, the drive for a cause. They needed to expend that nervous energy to find food for Doggie, to walk Doggie, to pick up after Doggie, to fret when Doggie seemed down, to fuss when, suddenly, Doggie appeared uninterested in a favorite treat, to forage for the veterinarian's telephone number.

"Do you believe in heaven?" Richie asked me one day. When I told him that I did, he said, "I don't want to go there unless Doggie comes along."

I got it.

In fact, just from watching people walk their dogs, I developed a great admiration for Americans' sense of duty and commitment. Being squeamish about feces, I have marveled at those brave girls and boys, women and men, who daily walk their dogs, a leash in one hand, a plastic bag in the other. Often, the bag droops with the weight of poop dropped by the dog and dutifully harvested by its walker. American dogs deserve credit for bringing people together, serving as veritable currency for social interactions. It's rare, in my experience, to see two strangers in the United States pause to hold each other in conversation. Yet, numerous times I have seen two or more strangers with dogs stop and exchange notes, talking excitedly, lovingly, about their pets' quirks.

One day I encountered an elderly woman sitting on a wooden bench near the center of Amherst, a miniature poodle on her lap. The dog barked at every passerby. The woman, to distract the dog, held it in conversation as one might a precocious child. "Be a good girl," the woman cooed. "Are you trying to be naughty now?"

Americans' obsession with dogs often became subjects of conversation among Africans. A Nigerian once complained that he found it impossible to eat bread at the home of an American who had invited him to dinner.

"Before slicing the bread for dinner, the woman began to play with her dog. The dog licked her hands. And without washing hands, she grabbed the loaf of bread and began to slice it. I couldn't bring myself to eat it," he said, shaking his head and body in exaggerated horror.

Another Nigerian, who had lived in America longer than I, told me, "If a dog and a human were drowning in a rushing flood, many Americans would first rescue the dog." It struck me as funny, except that the man who made the conjecture assured me it was far from a joke.

One day I met a couple walking their two dogs. They noticed that I took the trouble of getting as far away from the dogs as possible.

The woman gave me a reassuring smile. "They're the nicest dogs," she told me, pausing with the dog at the end of her leash. It was as if she wanted me to venture close and play with the dog.

I stopped but kept my distance. "I don't doubt you," I replied.

"But I'm rather scared of dogs. Or, as I like to say, they're scared of me."

The man, who had also stopped with his own dog, laughed. "These ones are really, really friendly."

I nodded but kept my eyes, warily, on the dogs. They regarded me with dim interest, their tongues lolling.

The woman pulled one of the dogs to herself. Then she bent over and lovingly rubbed its head as the dog sat on its hind legs.

"They're man's best friend," the man said.

"And woman's as well," the woman added, glancing up at me, silently inviting me to join the fun.

I did not budge from my safe distance. Instead, I managed a nervous laugh. They and I went our separate ways.

I had seen many dogs in Nigeria, but most of them were put to less sublime and more practical purposes. They were guard dogs, often caged in the daytime but unleashed at night to roam the compound, their growls and barks striking fear in would-be burglars. BEWARE OF DOG was a familiar post on walls or the metal gates that partially hid the homes where Nigeria's middle class or nouveau riche lived. On at least two occasions, such guard dogs had taken a nip at me as I visited their owners' homes. By the time I arrived in America, I had never been tempted to see any dog as a friend, much less a best friend!

One day, to my utter amazement, I overheard one woman tell another that she and her husband had decided not to have any children. "But we have two cute cats and a dog," she said. Until then, I had never heard children and pets so brazenly mentioned in the same breath.

MUCH OF AMERICAN TELEVISION disillusioned me. I often gaped, incredulous, at talk-show guests unabashed about dragging their best friends or family to the most glaring public forum to confess to all manner of secrets, from sleeping with two best friends to lying about their sexual orientation. News telecasts seemed to revel in serving a gory menu: drive-by shootings, suicides, arsons, and violent robberies. I saw the ubiquitousness of sex. I saw that, despite the vaunted gains of feminism, a woman's body was available to be used in selling everything, from cars to canned soup. I watched some celebrated comedians but found their routine jejune, often obsessed with profanity and scatology. Sometimes I wondered whether some Americans' lives were so denuded of humor that they needed to hire third-rate jokers to titillate them.

I found certain features of American speech enthralling. In Nigeria, many used English not so much to communicate as to impress, to perform their learning. Just like the characters in my early writing, Nigerians would say, "It's incumbent upon you" instead of "It's your job." They treasure words like aver, conditionalities, expatiate. Coming from a culture where English usage was a form of spectacle, I found the American English endearing—in its aspiration for a democratic plainness, its openness to innovation, its jazzlike musicality, its sheer variety.

But my take on American English was not all endearment. There was a debit side of Americans' impact on the English language. I began to tell friends that Americans had humbled—perhaps "deflated" is a more apt description—certain words that, prior to my arrival in the United States, used to conjure grandness or evoke extraordinariness. I'd say how Americans, single-handedly, removed the greatness from the word "great." And the awe from "awesome."

I still remember the first time I asked somebody "How are you?" and he said, "I'm great!" Was he as great as Alexander the Great? I wondered. Or was he great in the tradition of Shaka, the great Zulu warrior? Great as in an immemorial poem? As in Shakespeare's opus? I was bemused to hear my American friends (or simply strangers whose conversations I eavesdropped on) describe pasta or pizza or ice cream or some wine as "great." I heard an American describe a weekend party as "awesome." I instantly felt sorry that I had missed out on a monumental social event!

The day I became a citizen, several friends rang me to offer their congratulations. But the accent of delight was by no means unanimous. One friend said, in effect, that he hoped it was a good thing. Another asked how I felt inside. He was visibly disappointed when, rather than respond with monosyllabic exultation, I offered a series of hedges, parenthetical asides, and qualified happiness. Another Nigerian friend asked what I would do if Nigeria and the United States were to be at war. I would lend myself as a peacemaker, I said. He dismissed the answer, insisted that I must choose one side or the other.

"I don't operate by such bleak prognoses," I said testily.

When I called my mother on the phone and told her about being sworn in as an American, she paused. Her silence was pregnant, suggested a momentary struggle with incomprehension. Then, regaining her voice, she asked in an anxious vein, "Why?"

I could imagine her picturing her son as having mutated into one of those big, bad characters she had seen in westerns: a cigar-chomping, mean-eyed, gun-quick, bad, bad cowboy. If I had turned into one of those, then I was no longer the son she knew and loved.

Why, indeed? I had to ask myself. What did it mean, at bottom, that I had become, on that May morning, an American? Did becoming an American entail an obligation, as my mother no doubt feared, that I had "unbecome" what I had been before—an Igbo, a Nigerian, an African? What deep significance was I to attach to the oath's prescription that I renounce and abjure all allegiance to my natal country? Did the acquisition of American citizenship transform me into a human slate wiped clean of a set of sentimental, cultural, and experiential data, the better to make room for a new, uniquely American imprimatur? Was American citizenship somewhat ersatz, nullifying Nigeria and all that it had meant to me?

Did it call for amnesia about America's past history of racial dis-crimination against Africans, its unresolved legacy of racism, or the turning of a blind eye to the nation's sometimes exasperating foreign policy choices?

I had wrestled with these questions in the months before I decided to apply for naturalization. I had even agonized over the weirdly intriguing word: "naturalization." Did it mean that I was no longer Igbo? Or did it imply that my Nigerian identity had been rendered artificial, a mere conceit, inchoate?

These questions lingered long after I took the oath of American citizenship. I consider myself an ever vigilant, fretful American. Some days I find much to be proud of in my second nation. Some days I bring a more censorious eye to America. However, with the passage of time, the questions that once troubled me have taken on a less anxious pitch. Perhaps I would never find full, adequate answers but I decided to get on with life as an American, as best I could.

Even so, one question was settled in my mind. In assuming American citizenship, I had not undertaken to vitiate who I was before. I had not consented to bleach my "Nigerianness," whatever ambiguous meanings and stirrings that coinage might conjure. "Naturalization" has never demanded of me, in the everyday expe-rience of being American, that I erase Nigeria in order to enter fully and wholesomely into the patrimony of my American identity.

No, I have been able to cope quite well, even to thrive. I have come to see my US citizenship as far from an invitation to gain the kingdom of America by giving up filial ties to Nigeria. Rather than adopt a singular conception of citizenship, I have embraced a vision that sees it in terms of a fruitful marriage. As far as I am concerned, naturalization is not a loss-gain dialectic but a gain-gain proposition. In me, Nigeria and the United States don't find a battleground. Instead, they find a new momentum, a harmonic hyphenation: I am proudly Nigerian American.

Yet, this celebratory insight came only after the fact; it certainly would be dishonest to invoke it as justification for my decision to take up American citizenship. What, then, inspired me in that decision? Quite frankly, a messy mélange of factors.

Part of my provisional answer is rooted in Nigeria's historical experience. In 1995, when I applied for US citizenship, Nigeria was in the grips of a brutal military dictator, General Sani Abacha, a man whose operatives had killed several political dissenters, maimed many, and sent even more into exile. Some of the casualties were my colleagues or friends. I was deeply pained that, nearly forty years after independence from Britain, a cabal of ill-educated, morally inept military officers could hijack the affairs of my nation of birth and put my fellows and me at peril. From where I stood, then, the American promise of "life, liberty, and the pursuit of happiness," whatever its verifiable contradictions, seemed quite appealing.

There was another—call it spiritual—dimension to my decision to become an American. As a student of African American history, I had come to see the nation called the United States as already mine in a sense. My claim to the country was more than established by the blood and sweat of the Africans who for several hundred years invested their lives in building a strong America—while receiving little material recompense, acknowledgment, or gratitude. It was not difficult at all to imagine myself as an American citizen. The perplexing question was, What kind of American?

For there can be, it seemed to me then and seems to me now, many different kinds of Americans. For one, I decided that I would bring my African being fully into the lively equation of citizenship. Nobody who meets me or hears my stories or understands the values that animate me can mistake where I was born. Unlike the snake, I was not about to slough off my African skin in order to inhabit the American republic.

I came to citizenship with few illusions. I know that, whatever the color of the passport I carry, my skin, as the indomitable James Baldwin reminded us, always gives me away. I know about the perils of race in America, but I know of something even more potent and powerful: the grammar of values passed on to me by my parents—and passed down by all the ancestors before them.

Barack Obama as US president was not even a serious dream at the time of my naturalization. Jesse Jackson had run for the White House, and his exhortations had left many in the nation in tears, shaken to their roots. Yet, he had not moved enough men and women to that decisive mind-set and critical location where they could contemplate entrusting America in his hands. For me, then, the lot of many African Americans was still to be on the outside looking in. It was not an enviable position. Still, my reading of literature by African Americans, as well as my familiarity with their sustained critique of America's contradictions, led me to believe that the marginalized often have a richer, more complex, and profoundly more humane imagination.

These, I felt, were attributes that the United States sorely needed as, daily, its economic prosperity misled it into a false moral confidence and invincible certitude. A more intriguing way to view my citizenship was to spell out the challenge other Americans have, the partial responsibility they bear, to determine what value and meaning to assign to me as a brethren of theirs, a relative, even if a distant one. In fellow Americans' eyes, how American was I deemed to be, with my African features, my stories, my accent and all? How much of my Nigerianness would they permit me to bring along with me, and what would they insist that I check at the door? What price, in other words, would they expect—require—me to pay in order to authenticate my American identity?

An interesting answer came my way in an editor's response to the manuscript of my first novel, *Arrows of Rain*. In a letter to my agent rejecting the novel, this editor, although informed in my bio that I was a naturalized US citizen, nevertheless wrote the following words: *I must say I judge novels from outside the US with harder require-ments because of Americans' general difficulty in picking up books from other cultures.*

The editor's letter veered, by default, into the internal debate occasioned by my becoming an American citizen. I was aware that, once in a while, American publishers would issue a novel set in Africa but written by a writer born and bred in Bruce Springs-teen's America. But I was born and reared in Nigeria, and my novel evinces a depth of intimacy with its characters, setting, and events. Apparently, then, this editor could not imagine me as quite truly American. For her, my oath of allegiance might as well be a nullity. My ritual of naturalization was in vain. The US passport I carry was a mere accoutrement, signifying little. Simply stated, I didn't figure in her conception of Americans, a breed she maligned— unfairly, it must be stated—as culturally insular and aesthetically incestuous.

There must have been some validity to the editor's charac-terization of Americans. I don't doubt that there are parochial readers in America, antipathetic to texts by authors whose names sound "alien," content to subsist on the narrowest idea of literary nativism. Yet, there are many different kinds of Americans. There are many who are both adventurous and open-minded when it comes to sampling cultural products from all over the world. The problem did not lie in Americans' literary taste, which is often broad and capacious. It lay in this one editor's narrow, miscon-ceived mind.

What would it take to get that particular editor to see me, an American citizen who freely—indeed gleefully—reads books from other cultures, less as an aberrant phenomenon than an equally valid kind of American? Would she require that I renounce and abjure my cosmopolitan tastes in order to belong to her parched cultural landscape? Or would she be persuaded, perhaps, to adjust her vision and enlarge her idea of American citizenry?

On my part, I still wonder if my first reactions to American life tended to ungracious harshness. I am still residually uncomfortable when I hear the words "personal space." I still treasure friends dropping in on me without warning. I have adjusted a little bit to dogs, calibrated my relationship with those brave and complex citizens of the canine republic, but I still flinch when they are pegged as man's and woman's best friends.

It would be sad if I left other American citizens with the impression that I disdain their choices. At any rate, it is far from my intention. To the extent that some of my views appear scathing, it is due, I like to think, to the way my tongue is fashioned: a sharp, sometimes-trenchant, style.

In fact, that acidulous tendency is most fully displayed in my criticism of Nigeria, a heartbreak nation rich in promise and prospect but short on achievement.

I frequently run into Americans who have one grouse or another against Nigerians. Often, they gripe about being inundated with letters or emails from Nigerian scam artists promising millions of dollars, on the condition that the recipient provide confidential information about his or her bank account. The misfortune that befalls those gullible or greedy enough to be duped by the scheme is better left to the imagination. Sometimes, I meet Americans whose complaint is a blanket one: about Nigerians' haughty deportment, grating loudness, or showiness.

Blanket stigmas are themselves troubling, and simply unfair. Some Nigerians' negative habits also trouble me but not as much as the visceral temptation to paint all Nigerians with the same brush: as drug smugglers or credit-card fraudsters or just plain vain. Some Americans don't seem aware of the fact that, at about 170 million, Nigeria has the largest population in Africa—and the largest concentration of people of African descent in the world. And most of these Nigerians are decent, hardworking, and well educated. Many Americans also fail to realize that Nigeria is one of the largest producers of crude oil in the world and used to be far more important to America's energy needs than was widely recognized.

Sadly, Nigeria is also a country conceived in hope but nurtured—primarily by its gluttonous leaders and their global corporate partners in crime—into hopelessness. If Nigerian scams had made themselves felt around the world, it was largely because the country's leaders had respected no bounds or limits in their egregious grasping, in their culture of self-aggrandizement and illicit enrichment. Between them, two of Nigeria's former military dictators may have siphoned off as much as ten billion dollars from the country's oil earnings. Most of that money was believed to be in foreign banks or assets.

Despite the transfer of power to an elected government in 1999, Nigerians remained far from confident that such scandalous levels of corruption were in their past. These are painful conjectures and intuitions to have about one's country of birth. They are painful and also—as far as I am concerned—unforgivable.

The same year Nigeria made a transition to what is generally called a "nascent democracy," I accepted an invitation to contribute a weekly column to one of Nigeria's major daily newspapers. I have sustained the column, even though I have had to move it to different newspapers. Each week, I fashion a column that lacerates some of the scoundrels masked as Nigerian leaders. I pour scorn on the poseurs who dug, or dig, graves for Nigerians' hopes. I envision myself as a scourge of the mindless, debauched fools who have aborted or discounted the considerable promise of Nigeria.

AN AFRICAN FOLKTALE,
A WALL STREET LESSON

For several years during my childhood, I had the great fortune of being in a household without a television set. My parents simply couldn't afford a TV.

Of course, I did not know at the time how fortunate I was. Instead, I wallowed in self-pity. And, of course, I envied any friend whose parents had bought some black-and-white TV. My parents were dead set against allowing their children that idle time that fertilized dawdling, any form of dissipation. Even so, every chance I had, I sneaked away to some friend's home where I could watch the magical contraption.

As we had no TV, our parents and other adults frequently told us folktales. Many nights, just after dinner, my siblings, cousins, and I would sit on the floor, forming a semicircle around one of my parents, an aunt, or an uncle, who sat on a stool or chair to tell us a story.

I didn't realize it at the time, but the storytelling sessions were a marvelous postprandial treat. The folktales featured both human and animal characters, but mostly the latter. They were also of different kinds. Some were meant to foster moral acumen in children; these often dramatized the consequences of making ill-advised choices. Some were calculated to answer quasi-biological or mythic questions: *Why don't women grow beards?* or *Why does a Tortoise have a broken shell?* or *Why did God leave the world to make a home in the sky?* or *How did Lion become king of all animals?* or *Why do people eat chicken most of all the animals?* Some of the folktales were for old-fashioned fun, sheer delectation.

In many of them, Tortoise was a recurrent character. In folktale after Igbo folktale, Tortoise starred in one role or another. He was sometimes a protagonist, at other times an antagonist. He could feature as a villain in one, a wit in another, a self-destructive smart-aleck or an unlikely hero in yet another. Often, Tortoise was all these personae rolled into one: self-ruining fool and riddle-solving redeemer.

Each storytelling session had an opening formula. The story-teller would say, *"E nwelu mu akuko nga akolu unu."* (I have a story to tell you). We, his audience, would respond, *"Kolu anyi, ka odi uto. Anyi ga ege nti n'ulu ife I ga ekwu."* (Tell us the story. May it be delightful. We will listen to what you have to say.) Then the narrator would start: *"Olulu ofu oge afu . . ."* (Once upon a time . . .)

Sometimes, we would hear the same story retold by different storytellers on different nights. But each brought a peculiar stamp, some inflection of voice or other inventive quirk, that transformed the story, making it seem new and wonderfully unfamiliar.

Years later, in America, I began to tell these stories remembered from my childhood to my own children. Even though the TV was there as competition, they were transported by these folktales. I was so impressed by how my children cleaved to these stories that I decided to take the folktales, as it were, on the road. I approached my kids' elementary-school teachers and offered to come in and share African folktales.

My performances became a hit. One teacher would tell another how spellbound her students were, and I would receive invitations to bring my stories to yet another classroom.

One day, Deirdre Falla, whose son, Ethan, was my older son's best friend, invited me to share a folktale or two with her second-grade class in New Britain, Connecticut.

I told the students the first story would be about Tortoise and a feast in the sky. Since there was too little time to teach them the opening formula in Igbo, I told the class that I would begin by exclaiming, "Story time!" They were to echo my words at the top of their lungs—to signal their attentiveness, their readiness to hear my story.

"Story time!" I shouted.

"Story tiiime!" the students shouted back.

I began.

Once upon a time, a terrible famine ensued in the land of animals. The famine was caused by a great quarrel between Earth and Sky. Since the feud could not be settled, Sky withheld rain for several years. Plants and crops shriveled and died. The earth became too hard and dusty, so that nothing could be planted—and what was cultivated had no chance of surviving. The animals faced untold suffering. They all looked feeble, emaciated, and sad.

The only animals that looked robust, healthy, and happy were birds. And they were fortunate because they had friends who lived up in the sky. Each week, these high-up friends treated all the birds to a sumptuous feast.

One day, as the birds gathered to hold a meeting prior to flying off to a feast in the sky, Tortoise waddled up to them.

"Friends," he said. "I admire the spirit of friendship between all you birds. Pray, what business has brought all of you together?"

The birds explained that they were holding their usual meeting prior to flying off to the sky for a feast.

"Oh, how I wish you would take me along with you," Tortoise cried. "You won't believe how much I admire you birds and wish to be in your company."

The birds knew Tortoise's reputation for wiliness. He was a master at manipulating others. And he was always on the lookout for opportunities to swindle the gullible and take advantage of those who let their guard down. Some of the birds warned that they should have nothing to do with Tortoise. They wanted to tell him off straightaway, to ask him to ply his deceptive arts elsewhere. But other birds were already smitten, swayed by Tortoise's genteel manner and sweet, flattering talk. These birds were opposed to dealing with Tortoise in a curt, insensitive, and dismissive way. At any rate, they pointed out to their hawkish fellows that there was nothing to lose. Tortoise had no feathers and was incapable of flying.

"We would have welcomed your making the trip with us," the birds' representative told Tortoise. "Sadly, you cannot fly."

Tortoise smiled, for he saw that his charm was already working on some of the birds. "Well, friends," he said. "It's true that I cannot fly because I have no feathers. But that can change, I assure you. You're all very kind, which is why I always sing the praises of birds everywhere I go. Let me tell you: if each of you would lend me a feather, why, I should be able to fly just like the best of you."

The birds quickly considered the idea. Tortoise's sweet words had gone into their heads. With its beak, each bird pulled out a feather and gave it to Tortoise. Soon, there was pile of feathers. Tortoise glued the feathers to his shell. He flapped and flapped and lifted up into the air. The whole tribe of birds cheered, amazed at Tortoise's new flair for flight—and proud of themselves for making it possible.

The birds and Tortoise flew off, headed for the feast in the sky. Soon, they hovered over the great iroko, the tallest tree in the firmament.

"Friends, let us perch on the iroko tree for a moment," Tortoise implored the birds. "I just remembered an urgent matter I must share with you."

The birds were puzzled and a bit suspicious, but they had already fallen under Tortoise's powers of persuasion. As soon as they perched on the tree, Tortoise addressed them.

"I meant to tell you about a wonderful new game that some of the wisest people in the world recently invented. The game demands that each person take a flamboyant or funny new name. Before we continue on our journey, we must take new names. When we get to the sky, we will introduce ourselves with the new names we have chosen. Our hosts will be entertained to hear our new names."

Again, the birds were uneasy about Tortoise's proposal, but they decided to go along. They began to take new flashy names. "I'll henceforth be called Conqueror of the Sky," one bird proclaimed. Tortoise cheered. "Me, my new name is Celestial Acrobat," another bird proclaimed, again drawing Tortoise's applause. Other birds took equally boastful names: the Zipper, Faster-than-Bullet, Straight Shooter, Beaked Comet, Dazzling Wind, Ferocious Wings, Winged Meteor. At last, the birds turned to Tortoise with great anticipation.

"My name is All of You," Tortoise disclosed.

The birds were amused. What a neat name, some of them chirped. Their anxiety had disappeared. In fact, they gave effusive thanks to Tortoise for introducing the innovation of new names. They congratulated themselves on bringing along such a well-traveled, wise man. "We are so lucky to have you with us," the birds' representative professed to Tortoise. "Henceforth, we will not go to the feast in the sky without you."

They flew off again and soon arrived in the sky. They duly introduced themselves with their new names to their hosts. Their hosts busied themselves, bringing in a wide selection of some of the most delicious meals. In a moment, the meals were spread before the birds and their new friend, Tortoise.

Famished, the birds took their positions, ready to start eating.

"My friends, let us not be so rude to start eating without asking one essential question," Tortoise said to the birds in a stern voice. Then he cast a mischievous eye in the direction of the hosts. "Tell me, for whom have you prepared all this feast?" he asked.

"It's for all of you, of course," the people of the sky answered.

"I thought so," Tortoise cried triumphantly. Then fixing the birds with a grave stare, he said, "Remember, friends, that my name is All of You. You all just heard our hosts themselves say all the food is for me. I order you, then, to step back. I want to eat in peace."

He began to gorge alone on the impressive spread of food. Between mouthfuls of food, he would throw crumbs down on the floor. The desperate, angry birds scurried and fought for the miserable crumbs. When Tortoise had eaten his fill, he pulled a massive bag from underneath his shell. He began to pack up the remaining food, indifferent to the glares and grumbles of the birds maddened by hunger.

It came time to travel back to the earth. The birds were indignant. They went to the treacherous Tortoise and angrily demanded their feathers back.

"Friends, I beg you not to act in a rash manner," Tortoise pleaded. "Be patient for a while. Once we get back to land, I'll gladly return your feathers." He gave a wide, sunny smile, as if he were the most gracious being. But the birds knew better than to allow Tortoise to beguile them. Each used its beak to pull out the feather it had earlier lent to Tortoise.

As the birds flew off, the denuded Tortoise let out a loud, heart-rending cry for help. Most of the birds ignored him. But two of the birds turned around and flew to him.

"Please, could you give an urgent message to my wife," the helpless Tortoise pleaded.

"Why should we do you any more favors when you have been so malicious?" the birds asked.

"Because you're very kind. And, trust me, I'm a changed man. I'm so sorry for offending you and the other birds."

To Tortoise's surprise, the two birds reluctantly agreed to take a message to his wife.

"Tell her I asked that she gather all the soft things she can find. She must build a squishy mound outside my compound. She is to build me a platform made of leaves, pieces of cloth, and all the bouncy things she finds. Tell my wife I'm stuck up in the sky and must jump. I want to land on a soft mound."

The birds flew away, promising to do Tortoise one last good turn, even though they told him he was undeserving.

Once back home, they went to Tortoise's home and found his wife in an anxious state, wondering why her husband had not arrived home.

"We have an important message from your husband," the birds announced. Then they told Mrs. Tortoise that her husband wanted her to fetch all the hard things she could find and pile them outside his compound. "Look for rocks, stones, steel, wood—and make a pile of them. That's the message from your dear husband."

Tortoise's wife went earnestly to work. She soon built a mound, with all the hard things she could find.

Gazing down from the dizzying heights of the sky, Tortoise shouted to his wife, "Have you done what I asked you to do?"

His voice was faint, but she heard the substance of the question. "Yes!" she shrieked. Her voice was even fainter, but Tortoise could capture her answer.

He jumped. For a while, he kept falling and falling and tumbling. And then, bam, he crashed into the hard things placed outside his compound. A loud gasp escaped from his lips at the moment of the impact. His shell was smashed into tiny little pieces. He lay groaning, near death.

His wife sent to a distant land for a healer who came and used a special glue to stitch Tortoise's shell together again.

"Story time!" I shouted again. Mrs. Falla's students echoed my words.

"That's the end of the story," I announced.

Next, I asked the students what they had learned from the story.

Many hands went up. One said it was not good to be greedy. Another answered that we should not trust anybody who liked to cheat others. Another responded that Tortoise was mean, and meanness was bad.

A particular student caught my attention. There was remarkable eagerness on his face, as if he had some answer that would sum up the moral meaning of the whole story. He not only raised his hand again and again, he seemed to be attempting to levitate from his seat. I could not help pointing to him.

He smiled and composed himself. Then he said, "Next time, Tortoise should go up there with a parachute."

The response took my breath away. "Wow! Wow!" was all I could say.

The kid had sidestepped all the ethical considerations and gone straight for strategy. It struck me as a neo-Machiavellian answer, revealing a precocious corporatist sensibility.

Someday, I mused to myself, that kid is going to find himself on Wall Street. Or in some other corner of the world where men and women with Tortoise's mind-set head for gruel fests with all manner of armor, including parachutes—in case there's a modern-day feast high up in the sky.

A DYING FATHER, DREAMS OF BURMA AND ENGLAND

During a visit to my native Nigeria in January 1993, I saw signs that some dreadful illness had crept into my father. His spare body had filled out in a way that did not spell well-being. His face had become rounder, paler, a little sadder. When he hugged me, I missed the sinewy strength I remembered from his arms. He used to walk briskly, but his gait had slowed to the cautious pace of a man plagued by aches. His clear ringing voice was all but gone. His speech sounded unaccustomedly enfeebled. Before me was a father physically transformed, his body no longer able to support the generousness of his spirits.

In June, I received news that he had been diagnosed with renal disease. Thus began my version of a son's worst nightmare. The most graceful man I knew was beginning his final somber dance. In my adolescent days, I had often looked upon my father, first as stronger than everybody else's father; then as simply immortal.

Christopher Chidebe Ndibe was a genial man of noble bearing, and quietly brave. His own father's fame lay in a few simple facts. He was apparently a remarkable marksman, a hunter whose gun was the envy of others in the hunting guild. On one occasion, a huge monkey had established itself atop a tall tree in Amawbia. For hours, different hunters gathered and fired at the mammoth thing, which gazed down at them with something of imperturbable scorn. Finally, my grandfather showed up. He took a look at the other hunters and said, with playful derision, "You're proposing to get down that beast with those fragile guns of yours?" He then climbed the branch of a smaller, nearby tree, took aim, and fired one shot. There was a deafening report. The pellets from his gun stunned the animal, sent it tumbling to the ground.

Grandfather, whose name was Ndibe Ekweozo, was also a palm wine tapper. In his day, certain kinds of men were feared for being diabolical to the point of sometimes targeting children. Parents would often warn their children against accepting palm wine from tappers. But many an elder from Amawbia recalled their parents making an exception in the case of my grandfather. He was trusted as a man who harbored no ill or evil. He was a young-hearted man who relished spoiling children with palm wine and stories.

In his day, my grandfather had also been an invincible traditional wrestler, one of the best in Amawbia, his hometown in the Igbo heartland. Those who knew him told stories of his wrestling exploits, with special fondness for a comical incident that happened during one communal festival. In those days, a wrestler could walk up to another wrestler and call him out to a duel.

Cowed by my grandfather's wrestling prowess, one opponent had lost his nerve and pleaded, "May we wrestle tomorrow instead?" To which my grandfather responded, "What then shall we do about today?" Till my father's death, villagers saluted him with the statement *"Kaodiechi,"* or "May it be tomorrow," a shortened paraphrase of those plaintive words spoken by his father's opponent.

My grandfather's other claim to fame had to do with white men. When the first white men appeared in Amawbia, my grandfather had been one of the few young men adventurous enough to go away with them. He and his fellows seemed drawn by the economic possibilities promised by the nascent white world, complete with a new cash nexus. Grandfather had hired himself out to the British merchants as a hewer of timber near Warri, in Nigeria's deltaic region, some 150 miles from his village.

After a short while, my grandfather and his fellow adventurers despaired of working long, arduous hours for British employers who paid them little but abused them, physically and verbally, with glee. They chose to return to Amawbia and take up the interrupted rhythm of their pastoral life.

In those days, modern highways were nonexistent, and travelers trekked long distances. The day of their scheduled departure, my grandfather had taken ill. Unable to brave the punishing journey, he asked the others to announce to his parents that he would be home shortly—as soon as he recovered.

Months passed, but my grandfather did not return. His parents and relatives presumed him dead. In Igbo culture, the dead must be "buried," even in the absence of their bodies. A deceased person, unburied, was presumed exposed to great suffering, at the mercy of the harshness of the elements—whether buffeting rainstorms or sweltering heat. It was the gravest form of abandonment, one that incurred the wrath of the disregarded, vagrant spirit.

My grandfather's relatives did their sacred duty by him. They dug a grave, cut a stump from a tree, and threw it in the grave, imploring the earth to accept the log as a stand-in for the dead.

Days after the funeral rites were completed, my grandfather sauntered into the village. His reappearance created quite a stir—and a spiritual terror appropriate to the aberrancy. On some level, his relatives and other members of the community were ecstatic. But they also knew the dire implications of a dead man, a spirit, emerging in flesh and blood. They were caught in a jam.

Everybody who saw my returning grandfather immediately halted and turned their back to him. Done half in dread, half in reverence, the turning of the back was a prescribed response when one encountered a spirit—which my grandfather had become the moment that log of wood was interred.

When the journey-weary pilgrim reached his father's homestead, the old man—who had been forewarned of his "buried" son's return—stood at the threshold of his traditional wooden gate and used a hand sign to instruct his son to stand outside. While the young adventurer stood in the glare and heat of the sun, his father sent for a *dibia*. Part of the *dibia*'s office was to preside over rites of expiation. Such a ceremony was called for, a ritual reversal of my grandfather's funeral. Unless that rite was performed, my grandfather would remain, in his community's reckoning and memory, a dead, interred man. His subsequent appearance in physical form would be seen as anomalous, an abomination. If the funeral were not formally reversed, nobody in Amawbia would touch my returnee grandfather. In the eyes of his people, he would stay a dead man, a spirit. And nobody would dare welcome a ghost into the community of the living.

The *dibia* brought with him a chick and a scoop of the tiny seeds of an alligator pepper. With the chick he began to beat my grandfather all over the body. He threw the pelletlike seeds at the returnee, part of a spiritual cleansing regimen. All the while, he implored the gods to let the chick assume the evil, corruption, and aberrancy in my grandfather's body.

The rite completed, the *dibia* ordered that a fresh grave be dug. The sacrificial chick, now burdened with my grandfather's errant spirit, was thrown into the grave. A wooden stump was also fetched and thrown in, to stand in for a new body.

"Earth," the traditional priest prayed, "we implore you to take this new body as replacement for Ndibe's body."

The Igbo believe that the earth never disgorges what it has "eaten." So the rite of exhumation was a complex transaction. Since a stump had been buried in lieu of my grandfather's absent body, the earth was owed another stump—a symbolic body—before the returnee-adventurer could be exhumed and reclaimed as a legitimate member of the human world.

Once the rite was completed, my grandfather passed from the threshold of spirits back into the time and space of the living. He had—for the community, literally—come back from the dead. His fellows could now talk to him, touch him, commune with him as one of their number.

I once heard an account of the whole ceremony from an elder in Amawbia. He had witnessed the event as a child. It had imprinted his impressionable mind with awe and amazement. In particular, he recalled the great feast that followed, with much eating, drinking, and dancing.

With his "deadly" curiosity about white people behind him, Grandfather settled down to hunting, farming, and palm wine tapping. But his flirtation with the white world, however brief, branded him for the rest of his life, made him something of a legend. Fellow villagers celebrated him for possessing a smattering of English words, most of them insults that the British hurled at African laborers. Many an evening, after sumptuous dinners that compensated for arduous hours of farmwork, some villagers would visit my grandfather. These visitors craved linguistic entertainment.

"Ndibe," they would urge, "speak to us in the tongue of the white man."

Their entreaties made my grandfather eager.

"Bladder foolu!" he would say, his thick accent mangling the malign words and phrases he'd memorized.

His audience would clap and hoot and roar in laughter.

"You sukaliwagi!" he would follow up, the keyword marinated in extra syllables.

Another roar of appreciation.

"I willi deali withi you!"

More applause.

"Sucoundrelu!"

Applause.

"Don'tu letu me givi you a dirtee sulap!"

Rising applause.

The legend took root that my grandfather was the man who first brought English to Amawbia. Years later, after I became a well-known journalist in Nigeria, an elder in Amawbia invited me to his house. He invoked blessings on me with a kola nut. Then, as I sipped from a shot of schnapps, the elderly man reminisced about the provenance of English in Amawbia.

"This thing called blood is not to be trifled with," he said. "Your grandfather, Ndibe Ekweozo, was the first person from Amawbia to speak the English language. His first son, your father, then inherited the language. Even though your father only went through elementary school, he writes better English than those who graduated from university. That's why he has served for a long time as the secretary of the Amawbia Town Union. Now the language has been passed to you."

MY FATHER MARRIED MY mother in 1958, when she was thirty-three and he was thirty-six. At the time, any woman past twenty years of age was considered close to being an unviable spouse. At twenty-five, a woman was deemed dangerously akin to a museum piece. At thirty, forget it; few sane men would court a woman so old.

In fact, most of my father's relatives felt there were two grave counts against the woman he wished to marry. At a time when the "ideal" wife had her primary office firmly planted in the home, a bearer and rearer of children as well as the sovereign controller of the kitchen, Mother had trained as a teacher. In those days, many people were deeply suspicious of women who had consented to undergo training as teachers or nurses in schools set up by Catholic or Anglican missions.

The second—and much graver—count against Father's intended spouse was, of course, her age. Father's relatives asserted that age must have weakened my mother's womb, rendering her incapable of bearing children. Father had countered their plaint with the simple point that this was the woman he loved. This response scandalized his relatives. Theirs was a world in which the romantic notion of love was hardly countenanced. Love was alchemized into duty. A man who ensured that his wife (or wives) and children were fed, clothed, and had shelter had discharged the burden of love. At any rate, affection was far from a ranking consideration in taking a wife. The likelihood of the woman begetting children was the decisive factor.

Father was stubborn. And he cleverly devised a way to blackmail his family into letting him have his way. And this was what he did: he threatened to go to my mother's family, on his own, to declare his suit. It was, in cultural terms, a truly scary prospect.

In Igbo society, marriage is conceived and acted out more as a social compact involving two extended families than an individual arrangement between a man and a woman. If a man showed up at a prospective bride's home, unaccompanied by his relatives, he would have advertised himself as mentally abject. And the stain of shame would extend past him and terribly tar his larger family. Father's relatives had to forestall that shame. They decided, even if unhappily, that if he was foolish enough to insist on wedding a woman with a bankrupt womb, they would go along.

Like two truly smitten lovers, Father and Mother became scandals of sorts wherever they lived. How so? By doing the kinds of things that spouses in the crazed societies of Europe took for granted. They ate together. They held hands as they walked. They took baths together. They addressed each other, endearingly, by the first letter of their baptismal names: "C" (for Christopher) and "E" (for Elizabeth). But they did more; they used the same chewing stick—an oral-care device made from a twig—to clean their teeth. It was the equivalent of using the same toothbrush.

Poor for most of his life, my father nevertheless carried himself

with an air of assured nobility. He labored at his postmaster's
job with the cheery spirit of one determined that dignity would
never be foreign to him. He hardly ever raised his voice against
his fellows. I never saw him surly. He loathed self-pity in all its
guises. He was never one to bear his circumstance, however hard
and trying, on his face.

The news of Father's ailment stabbed me with sharp anxiety
attacks. A large part of my distress owed to the fact that I resided
in the United States, separated from him by more than five thousand miles. I was also aware that his illness amounted to a death
sentence, slowly, painfully executed. Nigerian hospitals, like much
else in that oil-producing country that had been misruled by a succession of military dictators and visionless politicians, are little
more than ghastly caricatures of medical care. Dialysis machines
are unavailable in most hospitals. The few that have the equipment are flooded by rows upon rows of patients lying in shattering
anguish, hoping that their turn to be dialyzed might come faster
than death.

The greater source of my anxiety lay in realizing how much I
didn't know about my father. I knew little about his life before he
became my father, before he and my mother married and had five
children, four sons and one daughter, myself as the second child. Of
course, my parents had told us, their children, many stories: about
their own childhoods, about their parents, and about that distant
time of their own youth, full of excitement and peril. I had simply
not paid much attention.

The reason was simple: the stories were often told in the context
of rebuking shameful conduct. I was the rebellious child in the
family. I was drawn early to smoking. I hankered after all-night
parties. I was a truant student. Worst of all—in the opinion of my
parents, who were Catholics—I was driven to sex.

Callow and self-absorbed, I felt affronted, diminished by my
parents' stories. I quickly mastered a way to distract myself during

those storytelling sessions. I would focus on some cheeky fantasy, often daydreaming about some girl with whom I was infatuated. Or I would think about the day when I would be grown and wealthy, able to live my dream life of prurient liberty. The particular fantasy changed, but never the objective—to block out the lessons contained in the personal histories my parents shared.

I did an effective job of it. As I tried to grapple with the news of my father's illness, I was struck by the paltriness of the memories I had of him. It suddenly dawned on me how sorely I missed the treasure of stories I had once spurned.

Visiting Nigeria in 1994—a more or less annual ritual for me—I made sure I spent long hours with my father, asking him questions. There was so much ground we could never hope to cover, but that hardly blunted my joy that, in the race against time, I had reduced my margin of loss, however fractionally.

The first blurry persona I asked about was the Reverend John Tucker, an Englishman who had been my father's regular correspondent for as long as I could remember. For many years, Tucker had been an alluringly misty figure. All I knew was that he wrote to my father once or twice each year, but unfailingly at Christmas. As a child, when my parents were away, I would pilfer one of the Englishman's letters and run off to a quiet spot to read it. Many of Tucker's letters were mundane affairs: a quick statement about his pastoral work, a report of the progress in school of his three children, something about his wife's job, an expression of delight at the news from my father that his own wife and children were also doing quite nicely. There was nothing in the letters that could lift the cloak of mystery that surrounded the Englishman in my mind. Nothing explained who he was and why he and my father had become friends. There was little in the letters to reward the punishment I surely would have received had my parents found out I was peeking in their mail.

In a way, the absence of clues served me in my youthful,

dreaming days. I invented a place for Tucker in my impoverished life. He became a symbol that bolstered my standing among my secondary school friends. It did not matter that some of these schoolmates spent summer vacations with their parents in England. John Tucker became my peculiar fashion of *visiting* England in the days when his country was synonymous with idyllic beauty.

In time I outgrew this quaint fantasy, but not my curiosity about where or how my father's story with Reverend Tucker had begun. They had met in Burma weeks after the end of World War II, my father told me. Tucker, a lieutenant in the British Army, had been detailed as the officer in charge of the Signals Platoon where my father had served for a good part of the war. My father was a noncommissioned officer with the rank of lance corporal.

My father was not one to rhapsodize about war, yet he took unmistakable pride in the four medals he had earned. Among the few items of memorabilia that survived Nigeria's political crisis— a crisis that culminated in the Biafran War of 1967 to 1970—is one of those medals, as well as his discharge certificate from the Royal West African Frontier Force, dated December 31, 1946. The certificate noted "one small scar on the belly" as my father's only wartime injury. Its final testimonial captured the essence of the man who, years after the war ended, would become my father. *Honest, sober, and trustworthy. Used to handling men. Works efficiently without supervision. Gives great support to his superiors,* wrote his British superior officers in the discharge document.

Educated only up to elementary-school level, my father was able to acquire from the war the necessary skills for his postwar employment with Nigeria's Posts and Telegraphs Department.

One day, visited by two Nigerian veterans of the war, my father brought out his lone surviving medal from the box where it was kept, like a rare totem. I was too young to make much sense of the three men's conversation, but I was impressed by the passion with which they shared their experiences. My father and his guests recounted their gallantry in such and such a battle. And they recalled the number of enemy forces they had, in their own words, "wiped out."

I was always proud that my father took part in World War II, the most meaningful conflict of the modern era. I found myself awed by the war's moral dimensions, the strange configurations of alliances it engendered, its geopolitical consequences, the sheer scale of its prosecution, and its gargantuan cost in lives. It was not until I became a serious student of African history—especially the history of Africans' struggle to reclaim their autonomy from several centuries of European derogation and control—that I began to see the war in an entirely broader light. I was shocked—almost incredulous—to learn that some one hundred thousand Nigerians had fought in the war. Other African countries, most of them under the colonial tutelage of Britain or France, also sent several hundreds of thousands of combatants.

Why was this fact glossed over in the major books on the war that I read? Why were Africans consigned to the margins, their role often altogether erased, when the drama of the war was narrated?

As I discussed the war with my father, I came close to grasping a sense of the great psychic toll World War II had taken on the African combatants. There they were, compelled to fight in a war that was, in the end, the logical culmination of a species of racism Europeans had planted. The same Europeans had used this creed of racial superiority to yoke Africans. In Burma, my father became a budding nationalist. "I was constantly disgusted at the way European officers treated African soldiers," he said.

Tucker was not as haughty as some, but he could not help carrying himself, much to my father's detestation, with that very British of airs, a mixture of detachment and purse-lipped confidence. It was the carriage of a man secure in his place in the world, affecting an easy swagger.

Silently, my father seethed. He considered himself far more

adept than his superior officer at using signaling equipment. By their sheer presence and attitude, Tucker and the other British officers reminded my father of his wretched place, as an African, in the world. While my father fought side by side with Europeans (and for the same cause), he was a conquered man, subject to the whims of his British conquerors. For sure, his life was less prized. He was a man whose world had been turned upside down by the English.

Deep down, however, my father saw himself differently. He saw himself as better than some of his British subjugators. The thinker of such thoughts is a dangerous man. My father was constantly on the verge of explosion. "One day, I angrily told Tucker that he had his rank because he was British, not because he knew signaling as well as some of the African soldiers," my father told me.

Father's brusque manner alarmed his African compatriots. "Many of them dropped their jaws in shock," he recalled. "They were sure I would be court-martialed for insubordination. Some of them even feared I would be shot." Somehow my father remained indifferent to whatever fate awaited him. As it turned out, Tucker chose not to pursue the incident. Instead, recognizing that his less-than-respectful subordinate burned with nationalist ideas, Tucker went out of his way to befriend my father. The two began to hold long discussions, often touching on the likely postwar developments in British colonial possessions.

Tucker assured my father that Nigeria, like other British colonies in Africa, would regain political autonomy soon after the war. It was a view other officers mocked, convinced as they were that Africans were little more than bumbling children who would profit by submitting to many more years of stern guidance by their European masters. Tucker's generosity began to make a good impression on my father. He began to reassess the Englishman. As he did, his mistrust of all things and people British soon thawed where Tucker was concerned.

The two men, defying the gulf of history that separated them, began to build a new relationship. Even in the uncertain time and turf of war-worn Burma, that relationship could bear the name: friendship. The British officer and the African soldier, in deciding to meet on an even ground, were saying, in effect, that the arrangements of history were subordinate to the call of friendship.

Their friendship was at once beautiful and, yes, subversive.

As my father spoke, I could see that his fiery outburst against Tucker had drawn on an uncommon depth of courage from within him, to say nothing of his disregard for the imperative of personal safety. The world of 1946 was one in which Father's kind was meant to be seen, not heard. Not heard, at any rate, speaking in irreverent terms to any British citizen, much less an officer. For in 1946, Britain owned Nigeria. And Tucker was—military ranks aside—literally my father's master. Improbable as my father's conduct was—in a sense, because of it—the two men would go ahead to become lifelong friends.

Back from Nigeria in the spring of 1994, I kept thinking about the meaning of my father's relationship with the Englishman. The excitement of listening as my father re-created his Burmese encounter with Tucker stayed with me. I decided to arrange a telephone conversation between the two men. I chose not to alert either man about my plan, electing the mode of surprise.

One day, I called my father in Nigeria and linked him up, in a conference call, with Tucker in England. It was the first time they were hearing each other's voice in nearly fifty years. I had pictured them exploding in uproarious excitement, perhaps too choked with joy to find words. How wrong I was.

"Hello, Christopher," Mr. Tucker said, with a calmness that would have been altogether fitting had he and my father been exchanging weekly conversations for decades.

"Hello, John," my father responded, matching his friend's reserve.

"This is really you," said the Englishman, a half question masked inside a declaration.

"Yes, it's me," my father confirmed. His solemn tone had the ring of a courtroom testimony.

Silent, I eavesdropped, as tense and apprehensive as those long-ago days when I used to steal away to a corner to read the Englishman's letters to Father. What was this slow buildup, this absence of emotion? And did Tucker think, for a moment, that I would profit from foisting a scam on them, that I would orchestrate a bogus telephone conversation between him and an impostor posing as my father?

"How have you been keeping?" Tucker asked.

"Very well. And how about you?"

"I try to keep busy the best way I can. Lesley has trouble with arthritis, which slows her down quite a bit. But she has a lot of interests that occupy her. How is Elizabeth faring?"

"She's fine. We are both long retired."

"Yes, you wrote so."

"But we do some farming here in my hometown."

"That's lovely."

They exchanged tidbits about their children, Tucker's two sons and a daughter, my father's four sons and a daughter.

"How are things in Nigeria?" Tucker asked, for the first time shifting the conversation to a different plane.

"Nigeria is difficult, but we continue to manage," my father said. He spoke about the popular yearning for the military to cede power to elected officials.

"Yes, sometimes we read disheartening news about Nigeria in our papers," Tucker chimed in." Then he said, "Do send Elizabeth our love."

"Tell Lesley that Elizabeth and I also sent her our love."

"I shall be writing you soon."

"I look forward to it."

"Okay, then," I said, hastening out of silence, breaking in between them, for I sensed them about to hang up. "Have a good day."

They muttered their thanks and reclaimed their quiet lives.

My first reaction was pained disbelief. Father and Tucker had conversed with an unbelievable emotional restraint, their voices controlled, their exchanges hardly breaching the genteel confines of domesticity. In my mind, I had done a mighty service to two friends who hadn't heard each other's voice for decades. At first glance, then, their calmness on the phone struck me as odd. There was no question: they had somehow betrayed my sense of how they should sound in a telephone conversation, the emotional pitch they were supposed to affect, given their friendship.

Yet, once I thought about it later, their reserve emerged as illustration of the character of both men, perhaps even a definition of the spirit of their times. There was a lot to admire in these men who, despite the seduction of the telephone, simply preferred to stay in touch through the rigorous habit of writing letters. I felt mildly rebuked by their equanimity, as though I had rudely disrupted the familiar rhythm of their routine. A few days after the telephone linkup, Tucker wrote my father a letter that made it clear that my trouble was not wasted.

May I say, he wrote, *how delighted I was to receive the telephone call from Anthony {my English name} some weeks ago and was amazed to be able to speak to you, as well. I would never have imagined it was possible. Will you please thank Anthony for his forethought and kindness. For days after the phone call, I was filled with pleasure to be able to speak to you after an interval of forty-eight years.* He underlined "delighted," as if, now safe within the letter, he could finally express excitement.

ON MAY 28, 1995, I inexplicably took the handset phone into the bathroom. It rang as warm darts of water pelted my lathered body. The voice on the other side was my elder brother's, John, far

away in Nigeria. He asked after my family, and I explained that
they had gone to visit friends. We then chatted about a few inconsequential things.

Suddenly John's tone changed. "Okey," he said, "you have to be
strong." He paused and I held my breath. Then he quietly unbur-
dened himself: "Our father died this afternoon."

Strange, I didn't feel any of the emotions and sensations I had
anticipated or feared. There was no tightness around my chest, no
urge to wail or curse, no sense that the world was unhinged, spin-
ning maddeningly, no shattering sense of grief. I felt only this:
a serenity that left me startlingly confused. I wanted to cry. If I
could, I would have demanded tears flood my eyes. I wanted to
feel some pain, the sharp pulse of pain promised by loss. If pain
would not come, I wanted to scream, to lash out at fate, at time,
at life—even to turn to God and, raising my voice, demand, *Why?*
Yet, I couldn't work up anything save for this deep, inexhaustible
serenity.

Confused, I thought as much about the suddenness and awful-
ness of the news as about my idiosyncratic experiences in bathrooms.
Why did I find bathrooms conducive to contemplation? Why was
it that, in them, my thoughts sometimes seemed to become clearer,
my imagination more vivid? Why, I wondered, did the meaning of
things come to me in the bathroom, my body bared, vulnerable?

It was only after my brother hung up that I felt a taut heaviness
settle in my heart. I desperately clung to images of my father alive.
I recaptured him emoting during an international soccer game.
Father was an avid lover of the game. Listening to a game was
one of the few occasions he would raise his voice, in exultation or
exasperation, depending on how his team was faring. I pictured
him washing his own clothes; a man of almost-compulsive cleanli-
ness, he never believed that his children could get his clothes clean
enough. I remembered him working on his farm under the sweltering sun, remembered the sweat that ran down his arched back

as he scooped up soil with his hoe. I recalled him kneeling, every blessed day, first thing in the morning and last thing at night, to lead his family in prayer. I remembered how he and my mother would always wake up at 5 A.M. to take a cold bath together, however chilly the temperature. They would then wake us up to say morning prayers. Thereafter, holding hands, they both went off to attend morning Mass. I remembered how Father would cuddle his old, cranky transistor radio in the morning. He would hold up the radio and turn it this way and that, straining to hear the world news broadcast of the British Broadcasting Corporation. Despite his efforts, many of the broadcaster's words were strangled by static.

I summoned up these familiar moments because I was loath to picture my father still, inert, dead.

It fell to me to call Tucker in England with news of my father's passing. He wasn't home, so I left the message with his wife. I was relieved that I didn't have to hear his reaction. In the days that followed, I spent much time thinking about my father's friendship with his former English officer. I obsessed over what their friendship meant to them, and what it could mean for me. On a purely practical level, how had they managed to keep up regular correspondence for close to fifty years? Even though I have friends scattered all over the world, I write to them, at best, in fits and starts.

Often, when I consider writing to friends, I end up reaching for the phone instead. Or I would send a text or a cryptic email. Was mine, then, a lazier age? A too-busy age? Or was it simply that technology has rendered obsolete the necessity for letter writing?

The hunger to probe my father's past was linked to my desire to deepen self-knowledge, to understand the clay from which I was molded. I felt certain that there were things his friendship with Tucker could tell me about my father and his age, and about myself and mine. At the very least, it would illuminate for me a world whose terrors and triumphs I knew only dimly, through accounts in history books. It would instruct me on a world in which the most horrendous war in human history was fought by brave men but also by the vile. The near half-century of their correspondence encompassed some of the most dramatic events between Africa and Europe.

What kinds of statements did my father make as those events unfolded? Were his letters silent on sensitive political issues, say, on Nigeria's postwar struggle for independence from Britain? For such silence would be telling, even if my father regarded it as a fair price to pay in order not to fray the bond of friendship.

My own direct experience of war began in 1967, when I was barely seven, and my country was embroiled in a fratricidal war that lasted until 1970. The war's images of famine, destitution, and death remain sharp in my adult mind. I vividly remember the throngs of emaciated refugees waiting in long, unmoving lines for relief food donated by Caritas or some other humanitarian group. I remember how many people would slump from exhaustion before they were able to fetch food. I remember women suckling their babies on flat, sapped breasts. I remember children whose bodies seemed sheared to the bone, their heads big and bare, and eyes sunken. It is a picture that, years later, became all too familiar, brought into living rooms in all the colorful accents of television from Bosnia, Sierra Leone, Liberia, Rwanda, Burundi, and the Congo: images of humans at their most hopeless and grotesque, as if death, in making slow haste, was withholding from them the joys of a grave.

The history of Nigeria, a country with the largest population of black people in the world, is a testimony to the disastrous aftermath of Europe's bold, but wrong minded, attempt to create modern nation-states in Africa. Britain, France, Belgium, Portugal, and Spain, in carving up Africa among themselves in the second part of the nineteenth century, paid little attention to the infusion of national consciousness in the freshly created colonial outposts.

There was no effort to redraw the map of Africa along lines that could sustain a sense of community among the subjects of these new nations, much less serve to strengthen national identity. For Europe, the overriding objective was to secure exclusive territories on the African continent for the promotion of the economic interests of individual European nations.

Nigeria exemplifies the tragic result of this cavalier, arbitrary, and profit-driven policy. The British threw together more than four hundred different ethnic groups and gave the behemoth a new name: Nigeria. The chaos inherent in this cartographic arrangement is best understood by imagining the forced amalgamation of all of Europe into one nation. From the very moment of its conception as a nation, Nigeria contained the seeds of fission. A volatile ethnic tension was exacerbated by religious and other cultural differences. These divisive tendencies attained a dramatic force in 1967 when the country's southeastern region, predominantly Igbo and Christian, renamed itself Biafra and declared its intent to secede from the Nigerian nation. Had the secession succeeded, Biafra would have become the first modern nation in Africa created by Africans themselves. Instead, other Nigerians, defending the integrity of a territorial entity wrought by imperial Britain, waged a costly thirty-month war that squelched the Biafran dream. Britain, much to my father's disgust, lent its considerable diplomatic and material muscle to Nigeria, thus guaranteeing the abortion of the Biafran aspiration. My father found another reason to hold John Tucker's country in contempt.

Although a staunch supporter of Biafra, my father was committed to a vision of social justice, humane ideals he saw as superior to the consensus of national identity, even in a war. He became active among a group of Biafran workers and citizens who condemned the excesses of the secessionist territory's leadership. They had written and circulated a petition rebuking the Biafran hierarchy for diverting relief donations. He paid a steep price for his idealism. One of my most poignant memories of the Nigerian war was my father's unexplained absence from home for several weeks.

One day, some somber-looking plainclothes men had come and searched around our home. Then, leaving, they took my father away with them. I still remember the day he returned, sporting an unaccustomed beard that both fascinated and frightened me. For many years, I had doubted the authenticity of this memory, persuading myself that it was a nightmarish dream. It was my mother who finally assured me that it was not a figment of my imagination. My father had indeed been detained, accused of mobilizing workers against the secessionist territory's leadership.

With some luck, I hoped, there might be a letter or two my father wrote to his English friend during the war. Through the letters I would be able to feel the pulse of my father's reaction as the war progressed and more people perished.

I arrived in England on June 10, 1997, two years after my father's death. It was my very first visit to that old country, the object of agonized longing in my childhood years. Tucker and his wife, Lesley, had kindly offered to host me in their home for a day or two. During my stay, Tucker would explore my questions, reminisce, and pore over letters.

At Heathrow Airport, while I went through customs and immigration, I noticed I had broken out in sweat. I was trembling with anxiety and exhilaration. My uneasiness worsened as I waited at the cavernous Paddington Station for the train that would take me to Taunton, where Reverend Tucker would meet me. Then, as the train snaked out of the city, I was charmed by the English countryside. I took in the wide carpets of manicured green that rolled away on either side of the train as far as the eye could see. The train's motion somehow gave the illusion of movement to the lush expanses of grass, transforming them into quietly flowing green rivers. Hillocks dotted the landscape here and there. After a while, the greenery would give way to clusters of brownstone houses, tele-vision antennas spiking from their roofs.

Two hours later (but to my mind all too soon), the train drew into Taunton station, in Somerset County, in the southwest of England. I alighted from the train, certain that Tucker would immediately recognize me, being the only black passenger descending at the station. I was pretty confident that I would recognize him, too; for, though retired in 1989 from his pastoral post, he had told me he would be wearing his prelate's collar. He walked toward me, beam-ing. His movement was sprightly, his athletic physique worthy of an old soldier. We shook hands, and then he turned and led the way. He talked as he walked, nimbly. Even then, moments after we met, there was much in his demeanor that reminded me of my father's briskness.

In the car, the thing he asked was: How old was my father when he died? He explained that the question of age was never asked of Nigerian soldiers in Burma because some of them did not know the year of their birth. Seventy-three, I told him. "Oh," he said, noting that that was his own present age.

Tucker's wife, Lesley, was a biologist and retired teacher, a lanky woman with sunny eyes and a ready smile. I was charmed by her passion for birds and other wildlife. I soon found out that I was not the only African visitor to their home: a pair of flycatchers, migratory birds from southern Africa, had arrived ahead of me in May. "They come six thousand miles," said Mrs. Tucker of the birds nesting in the front eaves of their home. "They come all that way," she stressed, smiling, "so I think they deserve to be treated with respect."

The first day I asked few questions, content to listen to Tuck-er's free-floating reminiscences. He recalled how, in 1946, he had passed up the opportunity to return to England in time for Christ-mas, choosing instead to travel through northern Nigeria as the officer accompanying demobilized soldiers to their home areas.

He talked with great feeling about a Hausa leather bag my father had sent them as a wedding present in 1965. His wife went and fetched the bag so I could see it. He recalled my father's proficiency as a Morse radio signaler in Burma, his mastery of sophisticated American-made equipment that other signalers found challenging. "Whenever the American soldiers were not around, Christopher was usually asked to be the relief operator," he said. "I must have sent one or two of the signals myself, but I was nowhere near as good as your father."

We shared family anecdotes. I told my hosts how, when we were young, my parents had made for my elder brother clothes that were too big for him. The idea was he would wear the clothes for several years, and then, once he outgrew them, he would bequeath them to me. The Tuckers laughed, and then revealed that they, too, did the same thing with their two sons, James and Phillip.

I retired to bed that night feeling a measure of inner warmth. The Tuckers and I had been able to put one another at ease. Even so, I turned and tossed, unable to sleep. It was as if I wished to dwell on the beauties of the day that just passed. Awake, I began to realize how natural it was that this Englishman and my father became friends, and yet how improbable.

Theirs was a friendship that breached several barriers. The most obvious was the ironclad sense of hierarchy in the army, perhaps the most hierarchical institution invented by man. There was also the taboo of race, embodying all the historical distrust between white and black. There was the line of religious affiliation: Tucker an Anglican prelate, my father a Catholic. Then there was the salient fact that, in the 1940s, Tucker's country held my father's in colonial subjugation. Were Tucker to visit Nigeria in those heated postwar years, there were many clubs in which my father would not have been allowed to drink with the Englishman.

What would my father have thought about this? I was impressed by the vast difference in social background between the two friends.

My grandfather had been a wrestler; Tucker's father had been an assistant keeper of printed books at the venerable British Museum, a polyglot who became the Chancellor's Gold Medalist in Latin and Greek, prose and verse.

Yet, the more Tucker spoke about his early life, the more I realized that, like my father, he had known grim privations. His voice quavered as he recalled the time when his father sold his chancellor's gold medals in order to see the family through a difficult patch. "It's rather a pity," said Tucker, noting that his father had treasured the medals. "I wish he hadn't."

Unlike my father, Tucker never saw action during the war. And just as well, he said. The Nazi attack on Europe had started just before he went in for officer training. Then, after his training, and "thinking I was going to start fighting the Japanese any moment, the bomb was dropped at Hiroshima and the Second World War finished," he said. He abhorred the horror of the bomb but felt grateful that he had not been put in a position to use a gun. "I thank God that, apart from training people and being trained, I had not fired a shot in anger," he told me.

After his time in Burma and Nigeria, Tucker had gone on to Magdalene College at Cambridge University, and then on to seminary. Ironically, his path to the priesthood had been paved by his African troops.

"Whilst at Prome in Burma, one day, sitting in the signals office, talking to some of the Africans there, our conversation turned to the Christian religion," he said. "Those around me were all Christians, and English was their main language. These men had discovered that I was fairly keen on my religion. This interested them because so many of the European officers and British NCOs showed little or no interest in such matters. So they asked me: 'How is it that so many Europeans show no interest in religion?'"

The experience opened his eyes in a startling way, he said. How was he to explain to these Africans the incongruity that Europeans, whose forebears had proselytized Africans, were themselves non-chalant about Christianity? Brooding on the question, he had heard "what I can only describe as a voice saying to me loudly, *You have got to do something about it.* No one else present heard anything, I am sure, but the experience, which was quite unexpected, took my breath away." He had started on his journey to the Anglican ministry.

Throughout my first night, I processed this strange intersection of biographies and histories, Tucker's and my father's. The more I juxtaposed their lives, the more aware I became of certain shared patterns, of the quiet drama of their story, the splendidness of their friendship, and my debt to their example.

In the morning, I came out of the guest bedroom in cheerful spirits, even though I had slept nary a wink.

At breakfast, Tucker surprised me with the information that he and I would drive to Lyme Regis, a coastal tourist resort on the English Channel, for a picnic. As we set out in his car over cramped village roads, he seemed to read my mind. "When I returned from the war," he said, "I found England so small, especially in comparison to the wide expanses of India, Nigeria, and Burma." We drove on for a while in silence. Then, slightly turning to me, smiling, he said, "When I was in Nigeria taking northern troops back home, I never would have dreamt that Christopher's son would one day be visiting me and my wife in Taunton."

While he showed me around the resort's museums, used bookstores, and shops that retailed fossils mined from the area, I permitted myself the fleeting fantasy that I was my father and Tucker was an unlikely friend I had met in Burma. I suspected that, had fate not interfered in the matter, the Englishman would have loved to be doing the rounds with my father. We later sat down among a bank of washed stones and other sea debris to eat sandwiches and to talk, touching on as many subjects as we could squeeze into the time we had.

That evening, back home, Tucker and I sipped tea while he answered my questions on tape. He had no recollection of the confrontation my father had told me about. Instead, he remembered my father as "very cooperative and very courteous and very nice in his manner of speaking, and a very intelligent person." He recalled the pain of the moment when he parted from my father and other demobilized soldiers headed for the eastern part of Nigeria, because he had been assigned to travel with those going north. On arrival in Lagos, all the troops had stayed at a camp situated beside a railway line outside the city. "When the time came for my departure, it was almost a tearful farewell," Tucker said. "I remember that, as my train slowly puffed its way out of the camp station, a number of my signalers ran full tilt alongside the track waving at me until they could no longer keep up."

My father's very first letter to his English friend was dated September 9, 1947. It was written against the backdrop of a sharp rise in nationalist activity in Nigeria. British colonial officials met the agitation with a stepped-up rhetoric that ridiculed the very notion of self-rule. Part of the vibrancy of nationalist agitation arose from ideas generated by World War II.

For colonial subjects, perhaps the war's most inspiring document was the Atlantic Charter, a series of declarations issued in 1941 by America's president Franklin Delano Roosevelt and British prime minister Winston Churchill. The two leaders pledged to "respect the right of all peoples to choose the form of government under which they will live." Africans took the document as a promissory note for their own self-determination once the Allied forces secured victory. At the war's end, Churchill, in an egregious act of revisionism, argued that colonial subjects were not included in the document's idea of "peoples." Africans, especially those like my father who had fought in the war, felt bitterly betrayed.

My father's 1947 letter was a diatribe against the British. *Yes, he wrote, we Nigerians as a whole used to be cheerful always and under all conditions with less money and amenities, but I can tell you that this is not true today. The cause for this is that we wake up daily only to see that our position, economical, social, or political, is worse than yesterday. We are denied all rights which every living creature should enjoy . . . Laws after laws are made whereby our lands and other God-given rights to the poor natives are taken from them. These make the whole population feel disappointed in our so-called protectors, hence every one here is now unhappy and disgusted with the British attitude . . . the flame of nationalism burning in the minds of almost all Nigerians cannot be quenched.*

Twenty-two years later, in the midst of the Biafran War, my father wrote a letter to Tucker. *The story of my family and my country for the past three years is a long and painful one.* He described *the pogrom, the blockage by air, land, and sea, and the war of genocide and total extermination of Biafrans engineered by Harold Wilson's {British} government and sustained by that government up to this day.* He said the account of Britain's complicity in the Biafran carnage *will make a sorry reading for a Christian of your type.* The letter's only hopeful note was the remark that *my wife, our five children—four boys and one girl—and I are still breathing God's free air even though much suffering and hunger have had their effects on us.*

When it came time to leave, I was deeply grateful to Tucker for the glimpses he had offered me of my father and of himself. What moved me even more was to see how two ordinary men had done extraordinary things; how they had salvaged something beautiful from the ravages of history; how, transcending their own narrow biographies, they enacted a friendship that could be quenched neither by distance, time, war, nor, for that matter, by death.

Following my father's passing, Tucker and my mother agreed to take up correspondence. Mrs. Tucker's parting words to me only deepened my gratitude. After hugging me once, twice, then a third time, she said, "You know, it feels like one of my sons leaving home." In the silence of my heart, I thanked my father and his worthy English friend.

WOLE SOYINKA SAVES MY CHRISTMAS

In December of 1997, Deirdre Falla, my wife's best friend, came up with the idea that our two families should spend the entire Christmas Day together at their home in New Britain. The plan was that we should attend Mass together and then head to their home for lunch and dinner.

I had no reason to object to the plan. The Fallas and my family had grown as close as a family since their older son, Ethan, and ours, Chibu, met at preschool and became best buddies. In Nigeria, Christmas was always the most festive, colorful, and social event on the calendar. It was a time when friends and families gathered to make merry. People, especially youngsters, went from house to house eating and drinking extravagantly and receiving small gifts of money, cookies, and sweets.

Time to insert an important cultural note. When I was growing up in a lower-middle-class home in Nigeria, rice was something of a rare dish. We craved rice, but most of our meals were riceless. Many meals were also meatless, or provisioned with the kind of minuscule pieces of meat that brought the mouth little satisfaction and much anguish, reminding the palate of the legendary portion of the orphan.

We deemed any meal that featured rice and chicken a treat.

In my parents' home as well as my friends' homes, Sunday was the day to savor rice and thick, tasty tomato stews prepared with chicken. Some families would add fish, beef, or goat to the stew, but chicken was the most common, the most desired. Youngsters, my siblings and I included, looked forward to the prospect of rice and stew. I kid not: the sense of expectancy transported us, lent meaning and buoyancy to each week.

I kept in step with the tradition. Often, as I drifted through the drudgery of many a weekday, about the one thing that made it all worthwhile, the redemptive part of the tedium, was to make it to Sunday. For, then, one's stomach would reap the culinary rewards of rice, chicken, and stew.

If rice-filled Sundays represented the crescendo of the week's epicurean experience, then Christmas was the all-time culmination. When I was young, my theological interest in Christmas was at least matched—and often surpassed—by the culinary excitement evoked by the Christian feast. My friends and I banked on there being an excess of rice, an excess of chicken stew, an excess of fried beef or goat. But chicken was the center of it all. Yes, and we brought to the feast an excess of famishment, a product of all our accumulated, yearlong dreams for rice and stew and chicken that had gone unmet.

I felt no need to specify to our American hosts that rice and chicken had to be part—indeed, at the center—of our Christmas meals. The overindulging in that set cuisine had been deeply indexed in my psyche. So much so, in fact, that I could not imagine there being a single soul on earth that would awake on Christmas Day without his or her thought going, with alacrity, to the culinary bonanza of rice, stew, and chicken that awaited all men and women of goodwill. The menu was de rigueur. If there existed any beings that didn't adhere to its unsurpassable delights, why, they had to be transients from Mars or something.

Nothing could have prepared me for the culinary fiasco that played out on Christmas Day 1997. And I have put it rather mildly. I had lived in the United States for exactly nine years. I had spent all my Christmases with relatives or friends who were Nigerian, who understood how indispensable were rice and chicken to the celebration. It had never occurred to me that anybody, on Christmas of all days, would choose mashed potatoes or lasagna or pasta over rice, or beef or pork over chicken.

We ate lunch at the Fallas; there was not a single grain of rice and no chicken. We ate dinner; rice and chicken didn't show up. Both meals, riceless and chickenless!

To their credit, the Fallas produced a veritable smorgasbord, but the absence of rice and chicken spelled doom for me. Pancakes and pastas and pork roasts and lamb and beef and mashed potatoes and knishes have their place in the world, but that place is not Christmas. And, certainly, not as alternatives for rice, stew, and chicken. Once it dawned on me that the cuisines I most looked forward to were not about to materialize, I had the equivalent of a culture shock followed by a mild to serious panic attack. If I did nothing about the culinary mishap, it would be the first Christmas in my memory when I had not eaten my reliable rice and chicken—much less gorged on them, stuffed myself until I could eat no more. No, I wasn't willing to grant that dubious distinction to the Christmas of 1997.

How was one to bear the trauma of a Christmas bereft of rice, stew, and chicken?

I pulled my wife, Sheri, aside and apprised her of my predicament. It was about 9:30 P.M. The Fallas' plan was that we should stay at their home, savoring drinks and desserts and playing some games, till midnight. I had other, rather urgent plans.

"We must get home before midnight," I told Sheri. "There's no way I'll let an entire Christmas Day pass without eating some rice. It's going to take too long to cook chicken, but I must boil and eat some rice. And I have to do it before Christmas ends at midnight."

Having secured Sheri's complicity, we gave our hosts some excuse and drove away. Once home, I dashed straight to the kitchen. I found a small pot, measured out about a half cup of rice, and set the pot on a burner. As I waited for the rice to cook, I caught our phone's answering machine blinking frenetically. Sheri and I listened—in my case listlessly—to greetings left by numerous friends, relations, and acquaintances.

I perked up only when I recognized Wole Soyinka's deep, resonant voice.

LET'S PAUSE AND REWIND.

I first came to know about Wole Soyinka when, as a secondary-school student, I read his satiric poem "Telephone Conversation" in a literature class. It became one of the first poems I ever memorized. I was charmed by the poem's irreverent speaker, a vessel for the author's acerbic wit and bracing send-up of a tight-lipped, racist English landlady tormented by the prospect of renting a flat to an African.

That encounter with a poem sparked a lifelong fascination with Soyinka, a writer who combined creative pursuits with a ceaseless crusade for social justice. His credentials in the two sectors were exemplary.

If Achebe—as I noted on the acknowledgments page of *Arrows of Rain*—"opened my eyes to the beauty of our stories," Soyinka has been for me a model of a different, but equally vital, kind. For me and for many other African writers of my generation, he represents the quintessentially committed writer and intellectual. In many ways, his life and creative work bear out his proposition that "justice is the first condition of humanity."

My first novel, *Arrows of Rain*, was stimulated in part by

Soyinka's disturbing prison diary, *The Man Died*. It is a book I first read in secondary school. Beginning with that early first encounter, I began to wrestle with the book's haunting message and challenging style which I found both intriguing and confounding. His courage, his deep distaste for injustice shone through in that first reading. Yet, as a young, inexperienced reader, I was baffled by the writer's attempt to map the mental landscapes and contortions of the psyche of a social being—a writer to boot—cast into solitary confinement. I lost my way numerous times in the labyrinthine circuits of Soyinka's rhetorical style. That style is marked by a rather liberal dose of ellipses, a tendency to deploy neologisms, and sentences sprinkled with rare, sometimes Latinate or arcane words.

My first reading of the book was an intimidating undertaking. I had a hard time grappling with Soyinka's tasking stylistic quirks. My unfamiliarity with the writer's references to myths, philosophers, other detained writers, brought its own punishment. Still, I never once felt tempted to give up, to toss the book aside.

The reason for my perseverance had to do with a certain intuition. I had a clear sense that the writer's moral fervor was in play. I was a child of the Biafran War, a member of a generation that a poet friend of mine has aptly called Biafran babies. That colossally costly war—or the harrowing prologue to it—was at the center of Soyinka's detention. As the war drew close, seemed inevitable, Soyinka had recognized the scale of the carnage to follow. Some intellectuals elected to remain indifferent or silent, or to play propagandist. Soyinka boldly condemned the unjust killings of southeasterners and opposed the impending war.

He undertook a self-imposed mission abroad. His goal was to enlist writers and intellectuals to lobby different European and North American nations against supplying weapons to either side of Nigeria's looming war. The military regime headed by

Yakubu Gowon was not amused. It saw Soyinka's advocacy as altogether quixotic. Nor did the dictatorship care for the idealism that was at the heart of the writer's audacity. The regime had the writer arrested and detained on his return to Nigeria. The author's account of that detention gave me an early sense of the price this writer—who was then in his early thirties—had paid for his convictions.

For me, one of the tender victims of the war, Soyinka's experiences and memories of the Biafran War represented a metaphor of Nigeria's blood-soaked, wretched struggle for self-definition.

Owing to Soyinka's sometimes-inscrutable language, I did not always grasp what was happening in *The Man Died*. Even so, I was sustained by an acute sense of the immediacy and urgency of the book's themes. On some level, I knew that the book spoke about—or to—my Biafran experience.

As the years passed, I went back, again and again, to the memoir. With each new reading, I was able to draw out more of the book's moral implications. But even in my first readings, I had remarked the book's brooding take on the plagues of raw power. I was also able to tease out what, I believe, is the fulcrum of the writer's prison diary: that we die, our very humanity slayed, whenever we choose to remain silent in the face of tyranny.

It all planted a seed in my mind. Over time, the seed germinated and sprouted into vital life. Years later, when it came time to try my hand at fiction, it occurred to me that Soyinka had helped endow me with a ready-made subject. I set out to explore the relationship between silence and the excesses of power. In literature and life, I had encountered myriad occasions where the predations of the power drunk were met—often preceded or enabled—by the silence and acquiescence of the bystanders. Why was it that, all too often, those possessed of power succumbed to the temptation to use it to degrade and dehumanize others? Why—despite natural assumptions about the inherence of conscience and a moral compass in humans—why did so many inflict horrors on others or lend themselves as tools of an evil, antihuman agenda? Why did those sectors of a community that should lead in voicing opposition to injustice—the broad class of intellectuals—often lack the spine to do this duty?

I realized that the issue was ancient and ageless, ever present. Writers as divided by time, geography, and experience as Sophocles and Soyinka had probed the matter, the former in his chastening tragic drama *Antigone*. That play and Soyinka's prison diary illuminated the terrain for my first novel.

That first novel's central moral vision is encapsulated in a woman's proclamation to her grandson, a journalist: "A story that must be told never forgives silence." I fashioned that sentiment to echo Soyinka's denunciation of silence. I sought to draw attention both to the rampancy of power abuse and to the repercussions of silence. Those who shut their eyes in order to see no evil, to denounce none, those who plug their ears and gag their mouths, should be under no illusion. They may delude themselves, but they cannot enter a plea of innocence in history's great carnages, its galleries of gore and horrors.

In failing to speak up for Antigone, the people of Thebes leave the power-drunk King Creon to send her to an early, unwarranted, and callous death. And that deadly event ricochets and boomerangs, ending up birthing other deaths and tragedies.

To many writers of my generation and me, Soyinka had offered a contemporary lens for recognizing the nature of the beast that besieges and dooms Antigone, the inflated egos that fuel the Creons of the world, past and present. To me, he also gave a deeply personal gift on Christmas Day 2007.

Tarry awhile, if you don't mind, as I dip back to October 1997.

Nigeria was in the grips of a dictator named Sani Abacha. When the bespectacled general first seized power, sacking a much-despised interim government headed by Ernest Shonekan,

many Nigerians expected that he would quickly spring Mos-
hood Kashimawo Olawale (M. K. O.) Abiola from jail and invite
him for investiture as the president, honoring the sanctity of an
election that took place on June 12, 1993. As events unfolded,
it dawned on all that the expectations had been rather naïve. A
coup d'état was grave business. Few, if any, army generals would
risk their lives staging a coup in order to turn over the reins of
power to an idle civilian!

Once Abacha showed his hand, a coalition of prodemocracy
activists emerged to oppose his usurpation. Soyinka was one of
the most prominent dissidents. Sensing injustice, he characteris-
tically disavowed silence. Instead, he lent his considerable voice
and global stature to the anti-Abacha coalition. The opposition, and
especially Soyinka's role in it, raised Abacha's hackles. The dictator was a firm believer in the art of maximum power. His regime
confected charges that the writer and his group were respon-
sible for a series of deadly bombings, several of them targeted
at soldiers. Nigeria's security agents received orders to comb
everywhere for the so-called bombers, especially the prizewinning writer.

Everybody knew that the dictator meant business. In Novem-
ber 1995, he had disdained national and international entreaties
and ordered the hanging of eight environmental activists, including the writer Ken Saro-Wiwa. To save life and limb, Soyinka
escaped into exile—for the second time in his life. He traversed
the world's capitals and cities, denouncing the dictator and offering damning evidence that Nigeria groaned under a tyrannical
ruler's boots.

It was in these circumstances that the Five College Consortium
(made up of Amherst College, the University of Massachusetts
Amherst, Smith College, Hampshire College, and Mount Holy-
oke College) invited Soyinka to deliver a series of lectures over
several days.

I chose to go listen to Soyinka the evening he spoke at Hampshire College. I wanted to offer him one or two words of encouragement and solidarity. I recognized the tragedy of being driven out of one's country by men whose criminality and knavery could not be masked by their false cloak of patriots.

I confess: I also had a less-than-altruistic purpose for going to see Soyinka at Hampshire College that winter evening. I packed the manuscript of *Arrows of Rain* with me. I was going to ask if he could find time to read it. Given the subtle as well as direct ways in which his life and work had inspired the novel, I felt certain that any critique he offered would enrich my manuscript.

As I parked my car at Hampshire College, it dawned on me that the request I planned to make was neither easy nor reasonable. Indeed, I was struck by its rank inconsiderateness. A censorious inner voice seemed to agitate me. It reminded me that, at his age and stature, Soyinka was once again cast into the hard bargain of living abroad, a hounded exile. He had to live in constant terror of a regime determined not only to squelch dissent but, indeed, to eliminate dissenters like him. Numerous political groups, governments, and universities made incessant, sometimes-impossible demands on his time and energy. He constantly zigzagged the United States and flew around the world to drum up global attention to the tragedy in progress that was Abacha's Nigeria. "Rest," I knew, was a foreign word for him. His permanent address, as he often joked with friends, was in the air—a reference to the incessancy with which he flew from one location in the world to another.

Soyinka was not just an activist in the glib sense of that word; he was one of those who haunted Abacha, akin to a five-star general and commander of an army that was at war with the ruthless ruler. My inner voice reproved. I realized that, in the context of Soyinka's regular political and social engagements, it was impudent to saddle the man with my manuscript. He would certainly be entitled to deem my request thoughtless and unbecoming, this voice cautioned.

I left the manuscript in my car. The auditorium was filled beyond capacity. Arriving too late to find a seat, I headed for the standing-room area in the back. I found Ifi Amadiume, author of several seminal feminist texts, who had traveled from Dartmouth College in Hanover, New Hampshire. She and I exchanged small talk but fell silent once Soyinka was introduced.

As he delivered his lecture, Amadiume turned to me. In a rueful tone, she said, "Okey, is it not tragic that a man like this should be in exile while Abacha sits in Nigeria?"

I nodded in agreement.

Once the lecture ended, I walked briskly toward the podium. Soyinka stood there, surveying the appreciative, applauding audience. He recognized me. "Ah, Okey, you came!" he exclaimed as we embraced. Then he said, "One of your professors told me at lunch that you've written a fascinating novel. I hope I can get to read it."

It was hard to believe. I told him I happened to have a copy in my car and offered to run and fetch it. No, he said, he might lose it. It was safer to mail it to his address at Emory University, where he held an endowed visiting appointment.

The next day, I mailed off the manuscript. Over the next two months, I would periodically ring his number at Emory. Not once did I reach him there. His secretary would answer the phone and explain that he was away in one US city or another but, more frequently, outside the United States. I would ask the secretary to tell him I just called to know how he was keeping, or how the struggle against Abacha was going.

A few times, Soyinka rang me back—from France, Canada, the UK, some African country. "I hear you called," he would say. "I *know* you're anxious to know about your novel. I'm sorry, but I haven't found time to read it. But I'm going to read it."

Finally, on a Christmas Day marred by ricelessness, there was Soyinka's voice on our voice mail. He wished my family and me a Merry Christmas. Then he said he had just read my manuscript. He found the work "highly evocative." He looked forward to talking more about it when next we spoke.

I rewound and replayed the message. Then I turned off the stove.

"You ran home from the Fallas to eat rice," my wife remarked. "So why did you turn off the stove?"

"That message from Soyinka is better than rice!" I said.

CRASHING A PARTY, CHANGING HEARTS

On June 17, 1989, a Nigerian friend, Justin Ononibaku, had driven me to Northampton, where I did one of my favorite activities: scanning the shelves of used bookstores for some treasures. Afterward, driving back to Amherst, Justin disclosed that there was a party that night at one of the residential towers for students at the University of Massachusetts. The party was for a Nigerian graduate student, he said—her birthday celebration.

It was the kind of day, bright and summery, that left me keen for the charms of a social outing. It was a marvelous day to dance, quaff some drinks, mix with acquaintances, and meet new people. Justin, who had lived in Amherst a year or two before I arrived, was one of my guides in matters of revelry. He had a way of sniffing out where the best parties were happening. He had a reputation as a party hopper. Since we were friends, I often went along.

"So we're going?" I said. It was not really a question; it verged on an eager declaration.

"*They* didn't invite me," he said in a pained, deflated tone. There was a note of sourness in his voice, a sense of resentment at being excluded by the mysterious, unspecified "they."

What was he talking about? He and I were veteran crashers at parties. We'd sailed, uninvited, into parties thrown by Ghanaians,

Cameroonians, South Africans, and Cape Verdeans. We'd been to a few parties thrown by Jamaicans, Barbadians, and African Americans. And we were never shy intruders. We'd sashay in and go straight for the food and drinks. And then we'd approach any cluster of women and invite whoever caught our fancy to dance. Often, the celebrants would go out of their way to welcome us to the party we had crashed. At any rate, we had a perfect record of crashing parties. We were always indulged, never repelled.

"It's a Nigerian party, is it not?" I asked. "At least the celebrant is a Nigerian, right?"

"Yes."

"Then we should just show up," I urged. "That's what to do. Nobody will throw us out of a Nigerian party."

For a while, Justin drove on silently, his face scrunched up, closed. I read his silence as hesitancy, even resistance. I chattered on, my tone swinging between levity and seriousness, my playful arguments intermixed with earnest entreaty. Our reputation as party crashers was at stake, I declared. If, for any reason, we would chicken out tonight, balk at invading a Nigerian party, then our party-crashing credentials would be dealt a crushing blow. We would be finished.

Finally, my barrage of words forced him to speak. He affirmed that, like me, he rather relished going where he was not invited. He was at peace, in principle, with interjecting his presence at parties. The trouble, he explained, was this: he was acquainted both with the celebrant and several others who helped plan the birthday party. He was eminently entitled to expect an invitation to *this* party. The fact that an invitation had not come meant there had been a conscious decision—a conspiracy, in fact—to exclude him. It was one thing to intrude on a party where you knew nobody, nobody knew you. It was a different matter altogether when the "owners" of a party not only knew you by face, they also had your telephone number—and you, theirs. In that event, he contended, the badge of honor might lie in shunning the party, rather than barging in. A certain awkwardness, exclusively on his part, would attend his going out of his way to show up at the party.

Years later, I saw an episode of *Seinfeld* that captured the humiliating, vexed emotions that Justin must have felt when he tried to convince me to discountenance the birthday party. In it, the show's eponymous star, Jerry Seinfeld, is left perplexed that dentist Tim Whatley has not explicitly invited him to a Thanksgiving Eve party, even though the dentist has telephoned him to get the addresses of two of his closest cohorts, George Costanza and Elaine Benes.

In the end, wavering between a near-crippling anxiety about being snubbed and a desperate desire to talk to some dentist about his injured, swollen jaw, Seinfeld decides to risk stealing into the party. When he suggests that he and George go together, the latter coldly rejects the proposal. Kramer, another member of the posse, is just as staunchly opposed to arriving at Whatley's party with the emotionally dangling, beset Seinfeld.

In one of the episode's funniest, oddest, and most emotionally charged moments, Jerry and host Whatley cross paths. The dentist chides the cowering, embarrassed Seinfeld.

I understood Justin's argument. He'd been cast in a precarious position: people he knew well had not considered him worthy of an invitation to what was, in his reasonable estimation, one of the most desirable parties happening that weekend. Yes, I grasped Justin's case, but rather abstractedly. On a primal level, I was desperate to go to the birthday party. It was as simple as that. I wasn't wearing his emotional shoes. I faced no prospect of shame, and I bore no burden of self-debasement. Nobody had overlooked or slighted me. To invoke the drama of the sitcom, I did not have the slightest Seinfeldian emotional stake. So, the more Justin tried to demonstrate that crashing this particular party would be untenable for him, the deeper my curiosity grew. I had to see this party, had to mingle with the crowd that had excluded my friend from its guest list.

"We have to go to the party," I said matter-of-factly. No, I was unable to marshal any argument that would dislodge Justin's misgivings. All I had was that declarative impetus, that not-to-be-denied desire to dance, drink, mingle—a hunger for adventure. I doubt that Justin would have mentioned the party to me if, at some level, he didn't entertain the idea of showing up or didn't wish to be talked into going. "We just have to go."

Whether in response to my persistence or his own repressed wish, he caved.

About 11 P.M., Justin and I arrived at Coolidge, a twenty-two-floor residential hall at the University of Massachusetts Amherst. We took an elevator to the nineteenth floor. The moment we stepped out, the boom of music and the waft of spicy African cuisine led us to the venue. Justin opened the door to a wide, well-lit lounge that seemed bereft of furniture. The music, now at a deafening pitch, came from a room to the left of the lounge. From it, too, came stamping feet, the revelry of voices singing along to the music or attempting the impossible task of conversing. We composed ourselves, slipped on our accustomed mask of confidence. Justin led the way, and I followed toward the open door, which was more than halfway down the length of the lounge.

Suddenly, from the corner of my right eye I glimpsed a figure on a settee. Was this some hapless fellow who'd been bounced from the party we were in the process of crashing? I turned to look, and instantly stopped, amazed.

Sitting there, seemingly oblivious to the chaos of music and dancing feet, his eyes trained on a book, was a man I would never have expected to find in that vicinity. His name was Babs Fafunwa. He was a towering figure in Nigerian and African education, often mentioned as one of the continent's leading authorities in the field. His reputation extended far beyond the confines of academia. He was also a prominent public intellectual, much quoted by newspapers and magazines, a constant presence on TV. Besides, he frequently contributed editorial opinions to numerous newspapers. I had never before met him in person, but I felt I knew him.

Justin, no doubt dealing with his jitters, did not notice that I had stopped. He disappeared into the dancing room. I detoured to the Nigerian professor, but now racked by doubt. Perhaps, he would turn out not to be the man I supposed him to be. In that case I would apologize and retreat and chalk it all up to an eerie instance of striking resemblance.

"Good evening, sir," I greeted.

His eyes stayed glued to the page of the book for a moment, a man who would not countenance an interruption as he coasted to the finish line of a sentence. When he looked up, his face had a warm expression.

"Good evening."

"You look like Professor Fafunwa," I said.

"I am."

"What a surprise to see you here. Are you teaching at UMass?"

"No, I'm in the US for a conference. And I came to visit here for a few days."

"So, what brings you to *this* place?"

"My daughter lives here. It's her birthday party."

I introduced myself. He knew me from my work in the Nigerian newspapers.

Fafunwa was one of Nigeria's most august intellectuals. Even though I had followed him and read about him from afar, I had formed the impression that he projected a constancy of values. He was the kind of person in whose company I took great pleasure.

He seemed in no hurry to wave me off and return to his reading. I asked how he could read surrounded by all the bedlam. He laughed hard, wiping his eyes. Then he said he had few options. He was too far past his dancing prime to keep up with the youngsters at his daughter's party. Then he joked that, whether he retained anything from the book or not, reading seemed his only option.

As he spoke, I sensed a raconteur's aura about him. He was a man stocked full of anecdotes, memories, insights. And he came across as willing to share his cocktail of tales with me—a much-younger man but always inquisitive, indeed myself an eager trader in stories. For me, for as long as he indulged me, holding him in conversation was simply irresistible. I had badgered Justin into coming out to the party, but there I was—for that moment—indifferent to what was happening inside the party.

I pulled a chair and sat across from the professor. Then I asked him questions or made remarks that provoked him to speak on this or that subject, moving from the vicissitudes of Nigerian education to the turf of politics.

He was in the middle of making some point, and I was listening intensely, when I became aware of a hovering presence.

"Dad, why not let him come to the party and dance?"

I looked in the speaker's direction. She was square shouldered, somewhat petite, and wore her hair in the kind of low-cut fashion I had always fancied. Her voice was soft, but there was something assured and steely about her tight, athlete's physique. Her father was dark hued, but her light skin suggested a Caucasian mother. I imagined her born and bred in the United States, as her speech had no trace of Nigerian accent.

"Ah, but I'm not holding him prisoner," her father protested lightheartedly. "He's *free* to go." And even before I rose to answer his daughter's summons, he had picked up his book.

I went away with mixed emotions. The professor had not held me hostage. I hadn't cried out to be rescued. I was enjoying the conversation with him and wasn't prepared to have it cut short so unexpectedly. Then it struck me: perhaps the birthday celebrant had intervened, not to liberate me from the tangle of her father's stories but to rid the old man of me, a pest with an insatiable hunger for stories. Perhaps the professor had refrained himself, out of a sense of grace, from telling his daughter that I was the one who pestered him, deflected his attention from reading.

I could not dwell on the thought for long. "My name's Sheri Fafunwa," she said as we walked to the venue of the party.

"Okey Ndibe."

I was drawn to her remarkable physical beauty but also impressed by some feeling that she was down-to-earth, devoid of fecklessness. I had arrived at her party uninvited, determined to crash it. And there she was, a genial host, ushering me in.

The party room was dimmed, festooned with balloons. Despite the dim light, I recognized a few of the dancers as well as some guests, seated, chattering away. The music reverberated, made the air shudder.

Sheri and I began dancing the moment we walked in. It was a sort of fluid evolution. I had fashioned a peculiar style of dancing, best described as the art of moving as the spirit dictated. It was a whimsical routine, and it demanded a large, free space. I could stand on a spot and sway my shoulders from side to side. Or I could roam a room, a restless, shuddering mass of energy. My repertoire combined various elements. I punched and spun and kicked and bobbed and jumped and glided. Those who saw me for the first time often responded with awe, amazement, or laughter. My routine was a sort of mime act with a comedic core. But this much was guaranteed: little that I did on the dance floor was repeatable. My act was less virtuosic and choreographed than improvised, free, and playful.

Sheri's party was a bit too crowded for my kinetic style. Not to worry. As we danced, I deliberately, delicately bumped into other dancers, forcing them to back away. Soon I created and annexed a small space. Within it, I began to display my routine. My strange orchestration got Sheri's attention. She bore a wide, amused smile. Then the music slowed. She and I closed in, our bodies sweat-fused. As we danced, we talked, shouting into each other's ear to be heard.

I found out she was earning an MFA at the University of Massachusetts, with ceramics as her medium. She was also the assistant residence director at Coolidge Towers, a hall of residence for students. The job came with a spacious residence, a living room, a bedroom, and a kitchen. I told her I was in Amherst as founding editor of a new magazine, *African Commentary*.

During a lull in the music, I excused myself to get some refreshment. All the food and drinks were laid out in the kitchen, set off at one end of the living room. I was spooning food onto a large paper plate when, from just behind me, somebody called my name. I turned to face Georgina Eze, a jovial woman that Nigerians in the Amherst area called Mrs. Eze. She always teased me about my amorous pursuits. There was a peculiar expression on her face: a steady mischievous grin and unblinking eyes that held me, accusingly, in their gaze. I knew that look well—from my mother. In my younger days, whenever I got into trouble—which was often—my mother would put on that disconcerting expression. It translated into major peril for me, meant that some illicit scheme of mine had been uncovered.

"Mrs. Eze," I said. My tone was calculatedly smooth, designed to counter her accusatory stance.

For a moment, her expression remained unchanged. She just regarded me, her facial features frozen. Then she said my name again, slowly this time, drawing out every syllable. Shaking her head, she pointed to her eyes and pointed at me.

"Yes?" I asked.

"I saw you," she said, again demonstrating by pointing to both her eyes and me. Suddenly, she wagged her finger at me. "This *one* is special. This *one* is not for fun."

I feigned confusion, even though I understood full well. In those days, not without justification, I had acquired a quasi-playboy reputation. I was fond of courting women who combined beauty and intelligence. Some of them were students, some academics in one of the area's five colleges. I basked in their company, felt buoyed by their attention. It was a phase of my life when I was too restless, too adventure-minded, to contemplate settling down with any one woman. My eyes "roved"; my heart hankered for the next relationship, dissatisfied with any luckless woman who had requited my affection. I was allergic to pressure from any girlfriend to get serious. I felt safer, freer, when I juggled several relationships at once, when all understood that little was at stake. Whenever any woman broached the idea of commitment, I ran 4-40—Nigerian parlance for a fast getaway.

My dread of serious relationships was at once ironic and understandable. I'd suggest that its root was in my parents' exemplary marriage, a relationship that inspired amazement and admiration in each town where we lived. My parents were models of fidelity and closeness at a time and in a society where public displays of affection were rare.

It was a different story for many of my friends' parents. They kept to their separate paths in the waking hours. Some of the men frequented ramshackle bars where they drank, ate, and retailed bawdy stories with other habitués. If these other parents commingled at all, it was at night, in the secrecy of bedrooms, away from the gaze of others.

As a youngster, I went through a period when I felt embarrassed on account of my parents' closeness. At one point, I formed the perverse opinion that "real men" were the ones who went to bars, the ones who were not shy about sharing ribald jokes, even with impressionable children about. Sometimes, I wondered if my father was a wimp. Why else had he embraced the ideal of romantic love, when many of his fellows believed that marriage was merely an arrangement to sire children? Why did he accept the Christian idea that, in wedlock, husband and wife became one? At the height of my strange anguish, I wished that my father would emulate the men of the bars, husbands who did not seem in the least averse to cheating on their wives.

Despite my infantile fantasies, Father remained constant, guileless in his relationship with Mother, unwavering in his love for her and for us, their five children. In a sense, he and our mother projected to me a standard of affection and commitment that I found altogether unattainable, even superhuman in scale. When I began to develop an interest in women, I looked to the "bar men," not to my father, for a model. I had never sat down to refine some romantic ethos. Yet, I had drifted toward being both a maximalist and a minimalist. I felt most pleased and comfortable when I had several girlfriends; and I ensured that, in each relationship, I made an emotional investment that was decidedly shallow, pallid, minimal.

Mrs. Eze was not going to let me off quite so easily. "I'm warning you," she spelled it out. "Sheri is dear to my husband and me. If you're not serious, don't go there."

"I just danced with her," I protested.

She set her face into that disconcerting expression. "I just want you to know I saw you." She gestured again to her eyes, to me.

"We just danced, Mrs. Eze," I restated.

I didn't fool her. Of course, I had an eye for Sheri; she was the kind of woman I was drawn to. Mrs. Eze, without realizing it, had just handed me an idea for a courting strategy. After eating, I sought out Justin and suggested that we leave. He was chatting with acquaintances and seemed at ease, enjoying himself. But he apparently still nursed resentment at not being invited. He agreed to leave.

I went to Sheri, thanked her for welcoming me to her party, but announced I had to leave.

"Why? The party is still going strong," she said, surprised.

"Yes, but I promised to look in at another party. And then I have to go home and do some work." I had no other party lined up for

the night. Nor did I have any urgent job to do. I was merely striking a pose, leaving the impression that I was busy, that I was not
impressed enough to stay, that I was something of a prized guest
at parties.

Sheri tried to persuade me to tarry a little before leaving. I dug
in my heels, insisted that I really had to go.

"This is a terrific party. I wish I could stay longer. But maybe we
can get together sometime," I proposed.

Sheri and I exchanged telephone numbers.

"I hope to hear from you, then," she said.

"I'll call you. Tomorrow, in fact," I promised.

"You will?"

"It's a promise."

A promise? I didn't call her the next day. Nor did I call the day
after the next. For the next six days, I didn't call. On the seventh
day, confident that I had branded in Sheri's mind the impression
of a busy, desirable guy, I made a note to call her that evening.
Instead, she rang me at work.

"I was going to call you today," I said, once she had identified
herself.

"Yes, I believe you!" she said, her doubt poured into the retort.
"Just like you kept your promise to call the day after my party."

"I'll explain it all," I said. "It's been a crazy, hectic week."

"I believe you," she said, unimpressed.

At the end of our conversation, we'd agreed to go on a first date.
My designs were the same as for all my previous relationships. I
would bob and weave and skirt around, the romantic equivalent of
the floating Muhammad Ali. I would fit Sheri somewhere in the
chaotic web of my relationships. I didn't care that Mrs. Eze had tried
to warn me off. I ran a mini-empire of romances, and my Oliver
Twist mind wanted more and more and more. My mission was to be
my father's ultimate counterfoil, the guy from whose dictionary the
words "faithfulness" and "commitment" had been ripped off.

I used to tell my friends that I knew better than to submit to the repressive regime of marriage. Yet, two and a half years after I first met Sheri, she and I got married. By then, Sheri had graduated and relocated to New Britain, Connecticut, where she had a teaching post at Central Connecticut State University. How our relationship metamorphosed to a stage where marriage was in the equation is a matter, for me, of a measure of mystery—and a story for another day. It'd be a lie to assert that I never saw it coming. I saw it coming, all right. But I also did my best, in a way that was often clumsy, and with what waning powers were at my emotional disposal, to fend it off. Each evening, I discussed the strange prospect of marriage with a cousin, Ejike Akubude, who shared my apartment in Amherst. It was an unusual colloquy: I'd outline the case against, my cousin saddled with the role of advocate.

One weekend, I traveled to see Sheri in New Britain, promising my cousin that I would propose. Once at her apartment, I lost my nerves. On my return, my cousin couldn't wait to hear how it all went.

"I didn't do it," I confessed. "I couldn't."

He grabbed the phone and dialed Sheri's number. *"Oya,"* he commanded, "you're going to propose to her now. Over the phone."

I spoke to Sheri, in words garbled enough to register my reserve and nervousness, but sensible enough to convey the idea I was suggesting we get married. She seemed surprised by my move—or perhaps perplexed that I would choose the mode of a phone call. Even so, she collected herself to thank me and to indicate that she was open to marrying me.

Then began another, more intensive phase of my anxiety. Why had I proposed without first discussing the matter with my parents? My parents treasured romance, but they also believed that marriage was between two families, not just a groom and his bride. How would they react when I finally brought up the matter? For that matter, how would Aunty Mgbogo, who had pleaded with me not to bring home a white bride, take it? Would she have a good laugh, amused at how I had split the difference—marrying a woman whose father was African, her mother a Caucasian American?

My sister, who lived in New York, had met and liked Sheri. Even so, she wondered if our parents would not insist that I take a bride who, like me, was of Igbo ethnicity, not Yoruba, like Sheri. I spurned her offer to find me prospective Igbo brides from the New York area.

Neither my sister nor I needed worry. Devout Catholics, my parents merely asked if my spouse-to-be belonged to the same faith. She'd accompanied me a few times to Sunday Mass, so I said yes. By tradition, my elder brother, John, was supposed to marry ahead of me. My parents ordered me to ask my brother's permission to enable me to go first. John and I had a long, good laugh—and then he gave me his blessing. Auntie Mgbogo was ecstatic. She gave Sheri the praise name Obidie: "her husband's heart."

In the end, everything worked out. Everything, that is, save my lingering jitteriness about marriage. I had been a lifelong playboy, astonished by my father's gift for steadfastness, terrified by the whole notion of commitment. I suspected that marriage meant a wholly different, novel kind of adventure. What were my options as a married man? What kind of husband would I be?

Years ago, if you'd asked me, and if I had been in a mood of candor, I would have declared that my father had disappointed all real men and me. He had been too steady a man, husband, and father where some men I knew and admired from afar were social prowlers—in fact, predators. Father had not lived by my creed of what a man looked and acted like.

Then, a few years into my marriage, as Sheri and I welcomed each of our three children (Chibu, Chiamaka, and Chidebe, nicknamed "the Three Chis"), I became riveted by a revolution of mind that had begun to take place inside of me. I became more selfless.

I began to enjoy cooking, for Sheri and the kids. I took delight in helping with other household chores. I exulted in telling folktales and other stories to our children and their friends. If I needed to stay up for the sake of a sick child, I did so without resentment. I became a student of life, began to learn the rudiments of communicating with my family—and the fine art of listening.

In short, the truth about my parents' relationship dawned on me. I had been the disappointment and failure, not my father. I had been the wimp, too blind to see the majesty of my father's example, too scared to commit, too self-absorbed to surrender to love.

I am struck by the paradox that, after years of rebelling against my father's peerless standard of fidelity, in marriage I had gradually, without at first realizing it, taken after the ancestor. There's another paradox. It has taken Sheri, whose heart I won after crashing her birthday party, to soften me from within—and to lead me, with few words but many assured acts of love, patiently, slowly, through several ups and downs, to this light.

✦ ✦ ✦
ACKNOWLEDGMENTS

For me, the joys of communion with family and friends rival the delights of writing. My wife, Sheri, and our three "Chis"— Chibu, Chiamaka and Chidebe—irrigate my writing with their boundless love. I'm ever grateful for their patience and grace. At 91, my mother, E., remains a marvel of vitality, fueling my siblings and me with her unflagging affection and prayers. My late father, C., remains a deep presence, a dependable guardian angel. My brothers and sister—John, JC, Ogii, Ifeoma—are priceless treasures, reminding me that to love richly and be richly loved is to have every good thing. I celebrate my mother-in-law, Doris Fafunwa, for being a source of succor and good humor.

I am indebted to many mentors, friends, and colleagues who spurred this work in one way or another. They include John Edgar Wideman, Ngũgĩ wa Thiong'o, Wole Soyinka, Stephen Clingman, Ekwueme Michael Thelwell, Bill Strickland, Abdulaziz Ude, Clarence Reynolds, Okey and Hadiza Anueyiagu, Nana-Ama Danquah, Joshua Wolf Shenk, Kitty Axelson, Barbara Love, Chris Ikeanyi, Anani Dzidzienyo, Kango Lare-Lantone, Lenny Kindstrom, Tijan Sallah, Radha Radhakrishnan, Alessandra di Maio, Abioseh Porter, Ian Mayo-Smith, Krishna Sondhi, Christine Ohale, Cheryl Sterling, Obi Enweze, Lloyd Thomas, Bart Nnaji, Joyce Ashuntantang,

Ugo Ubili, and three inspiring ancestors: Kofi Awoonor, Chinua Achebe, and Aliu Babatunde Fafunwa.

It's a great fortune to have Emma Sweeney in my corner, as my agent. Mark Doten confirmed my initial judgment of him as an insightful editor, a writer's dream. I'm lucky to count on the vigor, passion, and energy of other members of Team Soho.

Finally, I raise a hand of gratitude to the readers who, embracing my books, requite the labor of writing. I'm enriched, invigorated by my readers' responses.